HOW DO YOU SPELL WIN?

MEMOIRS FROM A MENTOR

Robert Crook Collins
with Dena Chapman

Disclaimer:
These are my memories, from my perspective, and I have tried
to represent events as faithfully as possible.

Copyright © 2020 Robert Crook Collins

To request permission,
contact the publisher at dori@district-outreach.com

ISBN 978-0-578-85452-6

First paperback edition February 2021

Editor & Co-Author: Dena Chapman
Manager: Dori Collins
Cover art & Layout: Charles R. Collins, III (www.azure77.com)

Publisher: District Outreach Initiatives
429 East Oakwood Blvd, GND
Chicago IL. 60653
312/778-2579

www.HowDoYouSpellWin.com

CONTENTS

ABOUT THE AUTHOR
ROBERT CROOK COLLINS

Robert Crook Collins is passionate about two things: his family and mentoring young people to do and be their very best.

Rigorous athletics and a solid education carried Robert from being just another kid growing up on the south side of Chicago, to teacher, coach, Division I Athletics Director and now author. Robert has felt the realization of his life's assignment through the many positive responses and experiences from the young people he encountered while mentoring.

"God has given each of us many gifts, and a purpose and I'm so thankful for my assignment!"

How Do You Spell Win? is Robert Collins' memoir and the first book he's authored. Robert is the proud parent of four adult-children: Bobby, Dori, Paige and Ria. In his leisure time, Robert enjoys a multitude of pastimes including daily workouts and pilates, golfing, cooking and serving others through church ministry.

INTRODUCTION

I'll never forget the first day of my professional career and how it framed my future. It was August 1971 and I had just graduated from Tennessee State University. I had only a few days to pack up my belongings, and get back to Chicago so I could realize my dream of becoming a physical education teacher with the Chicago Board of Education. Having submitted my application in June (approximately two months earlier), I anxiously awaited my notification. Timing is everything. As soon as I arrived home, I received a phone call from Dr. Otho M. Robinson, a top administrator with the Chicago Board of Education personnel, to report to the Board the very next day. A feeling of confidence swept over me- I just may get an assignment, I thought. I met with Dr. Robinson and after a brief interview, he informed me that I was lucky enough to be offered the last available position. Next, I was sent to the personnel office where I was assigned to alternate between two schools, Avalon Park Elementary and Paul Revere, both on the south side of Chicago.

That first day started as I arrived at Avalon Park Elementary School where the principal eagerly greeted me with robust enthusiasm- administrators at elementary schools were always glad to see male instructors (a role typically dominated by women); they relied on male instructors to discipline young boys when needed. With a huge smile, the principal said, "Mr. Collins, let me show you to the gymnasium." I had never been called Mr. Collins before, so I thought for a quick second my dad was in the room. Nope! It was actually me he was speaking to. Before we arrived at the gym, three young eighth grade boys literally ran up to us and stopped us in our tracks to ask a question. "Are you our new Coach?" Not teacher, mind you, but Coach. I looked at the principal and he shrugged his shoulders as if to say, "Well, that's on you." I never responded to the boys' question- it was a moment of reflection for me. What does it mean to coach young people? My first thought was, yes, this is something I could definitely do, no problem. It wasn't until many years later that I began to really understand and appreciate the impact that my experience and wisdom would have on the young people that I took under my wing.

Clark"Smokey"Morgan was one of the three eighth grade boys that I met on that day and also one of the first boys I actually mentored. He was a curious and inquisitive kid; he had so many questions. When will we practice? How will we play? What I began to realize was that Smokey was a leader. He quickly became the captain of the basketball team. Smokey was short and stocky; he didn't have the typical tall and lean basketball player frame, but he had a very high basketball IQ for an 8th grader; he knew how to use his size by using his head. Most skills that I began to teach, Smokey easily and quickly picked up the methods and then helped his teammates grasp the skill; he was naturally a coach on the floor at practice and at games. He actually made my job easier, and any coach will tell you, a point guard with leadership skills was invaluable. Smokey was special. Like Smokey, I had questions as well- I wondered how he acquired the nickname "Smokey." So, one day I asked him. He shared that as a very small child growing up in the Cabrini Green Housing projects, his Auntie said he was a handsome, dark chocolate lil boy, so dark that he reminded her of smoke! That comparison turned into the nickname Smokey- and it stuck!

As I look back, those moments of my first day were extremely significant and eye opening for me. I had never been called Mr. Collins and consequently, I had never considered myself as anyone's coach, but all of a sudden I was both. Being called Coach resonated with me; it made me think about my mentors and professors and the fact that they had prepared me for this moment. My professors in Physical Education were great coaches with outstanding backgrounds and tremendous expertise in coaching and teaching. They emphasized organization and being prepared for the task at hand. As a result, I was very confident in my ability to do my job.

From my college graduation, to my first real interview and then actually receiving my first job offer, things were coming together for me; my life purpose was beginning to take shape and I felt a tremendous amount of joy, yet also a great sense of responsibility.

Dragging those boys around everywhere with me came with some consequences. I tore up my cars and I couldn't keep a girlfriend, because of the commitment I had to those young people. I'm not complaining. I loved every moment of it! For the next four years, we won close to 300 games and many championships. Those early experiences in my life drove me to my true career and the thing I am most passionate about: coaching, teaching and mentoring. Coaching, teaching and mentoring young people became my purpose in life. I discovered that it was the best way for me to guide, serve and help develop young people on and off the playing fields. I finally found my niche in life.

If winning in life inspires you, follow along with me as I show you how my lived experiences shaped my future and allowed me and the young people I mentored to Win (and sometimes lose) in order to understand and grow through life's ups and downs. The stories you are about to hear come from my youth experiences, high school, college coaching and as an athletics administrator.

Striving to be your best is a win in itself and my fundamental philosophy for coaching and mentoring. When we give our young people the best of ourselves, our best knowledge coupled with the wisdom of our experience, we are shaping future leaders; we are grooming WINNERS. Eat, breathe, and sleep the notion of winning. Winning is everything! Always and in all ways, well I'll say it, this is how I spell win.

CHAPTER I
MY STARTING LINE-UP

It all started for me in West Chesterfield, a small, south side community of Chicago; I was born and raised there for the first ten years of my life. The small duplex was located at 9217 South Dunbar Court, and there was a North Dunbar Court on the opposite end of the block - they were sandwiched between 92nd and 93rd street, flanked by Forest and Prairie Avenue. There were houses all around the perimeter of the block and court-way. Most people in the surrounding blocks never really knew where the court-way was because it was kinda tucked away, a little secluded I'd say. The people who lived in the court-way were proud, upstanding residents. They took great care to cut their lawns and trim their hedges. They didn't have much, but they thought it was important to present themselves with dignity and keep up a clean community.

Our first home meant a lot to my parents. My dad used the GI Bill (a Federal Government grant that provided relief to WWII soldiers) to purchase our first home. My parents, Charles and

DeLois, were proud people; they had survived some rocky, post war times, but now they were first-time homeowners and that carried a great sense of pride for a young African American family- a huge win for sure. I learned from their great example the value of perseverance and sacrifice; they taught me to be resourceful, but also that it's okay to ask for help when you need it.

My parents would often say, "Where there is a will, there is a way." To this day, I still believe in, and more importantly, live by this philosophy; it has always had the flavor of *winning* attached to it.

The court-way was different from most streets that some of my friends lived near; it was shaped like an old-fashioned keyhole; with a narrow entrance for about forty yards and then it opened up and it was round at the deepest part. There were six homes that faced the court-way where parents could watch their kids from their living room window. Back-in-the-day, it takes a village to raise a child philosophy was in full effect; all of the parents on the block made it their responsibility to keep a watchful eye on all of the kids on the block regardless if they were their own child or not. For example,if Mrs. Lewis, my first best friend Wally's mother saw me do something questionable, I guarantee you, my mom knew about it immediately.

The court-way was very unique because the surface was all rocks and broken concrete. Despite all its flaws, the court-way was the center of everything on the block for us kids; it was our field of dreams. We played ball and hide and go seek late weekend evenings til dusk. When the street lights came on, that meant game over and get in the house! Our baseball field was defined by four sewers that served as our bases and when you stood on base during a game, the foul sewer smell drifted into the air. Distant sidewalks marked the home run area, and we all kept track of how many home runs we hit that summer. My brother Chuckie and a few older boys won that contest, but even as a small boy I was swinging for the fences, trying to WIN! It's amazing how a space so small could provide all that we needed. We loved that place and I felt like it loved us back; it was always there for us.

Both my parents worked hard to make ends meet and afford a good quality of life for our family. The planning, insight and the preparedness of my parents has provided me a great blueprint for winning in life! I can't think of anything my parents did or said to make life anything but awesome for me as a child and young adult.

My Mom, De Lois Charles Collins, was probably the smartest person I've ever known. Yes, her middle name was Charles, as my grandfather wanted a boy so bad that he gave her his first name as her middle name. She was small in stature, probably weighed about 115 pounds or so, and never gained weight her entire life. She was beautiful, charismatic and a well-dressed woman. For two consecutive years, she was named one of the ten best dressed African American Women in Chicago. She ate healthy, and lived life to the fullest.

Her father was her biggest champion in life (she was his only daughter). My mom attended Burke Elementary and Parker High School. At that time, these schools were considered to be the "better schools." She was determined to receive the full benefits of a good education. She attended the University of Wisconsin in Madison, where she majored in French and Economics. My mom made the Dean's List upon completion of her program and to this day, she remains the youngest graduate (at 19 years old) in their history; she completed her undergraduate degree within three years. While in high school, my mother managed her father's insurance business. She built her own court reporting agency and eventually pursued a mortician's license. She became a funeral director while raising two very active boys! Her impact on my thinking was powerful. Personally, I never doubted that I would graduate from college. However, being an average student, who also juggled sports and an active social life, I suspect that my parents may have had some doubts. I recall the day when I asked my mom's advice about whether or not to pursue my dream of playing Major League Baseball or use my diploma to become a teacher. Baseball had teased me with being considered a possible draft pick by the Cincinnati Reds and the Oakland Athletics. I knew I was good enough, but at that time being good enough didn't cut it; you had to be twice as good to make the Major Leagues, and even then, there were no guarantees. After a brief discussion with my mom, she told me to call her back when I had made my decision. That was the day my mother willed me to become my own man and make my own decisions. It's no surprise that I chose teaching as my vocation in life; my mom had instilled in me the value of an education. It was probably the best decision and greatest win of my life.

My dad, Charles Robert Collins I, was a Lieutenant during World War II, and during his tour of duty, he received two very distinguished medals - a Purple Heart and the Bronze Star. He was an amazing man, person and dad. He had dreams to be a pharmacist, but being the oldest child back then, it was hard for him to fulfill his dream because he had to make sacrifices so his younger sister could attend school.

My dad was versatile and had many skills, one of which was dealing with people. He had that personality that made you feel comfortable in his presence; my dad was warm, sincere and empathetic. I'd also say he was very much an opportunist. I don't believe he ever really wanted to be a mortician, but after meeting his bride-to-be, his fate was sealed. My mom was the daughter of prominent Funeral Director, Charles Crook. She fell in love with my dad, and eventually Mr. Crook made my dad the assistant manager of Crook Funeral Home, one of the first African American funeral homes in Chicago. Crook Funeral Home was built from the ground up and it was the only funeral home that provided ambulance service. While working other odd jobs (i.e. short order cook and pharmacy delivery driver), my dad attended Worsham College in pursuit of his funeral director's license. He was a hard worker-very consistent and heavily involved in church ministry, spending time with his cronies (his social group), and helping out with many other civic groups and organizations that he supported. My dad would give you the shirt off his back; he was a giver, always helping somebody in some form or fashion. That's just who he was.

I am so very proud of my parents and the impact they had not only on my life but on so many people they encountered. And although my parents are long gone from this earth, their example of strong work ethic coupled with wisdom continues to guide me as I walk through life.

Ms Lula Thomas, nanny for the Collins boys, her role was extremely important to our development.

My brother, Charles Robert Collins II,(aka Chuckie) is four years older than me-my parents planned that gap so we could both go to college and not have the financial strain of two kids in college at the same time. Chuckie was actually a small guy, about 115 pounds and a wrestler on a city championship team his senior year. I remember being about 145 pounds at that point. I was always a little larger in stature than him, but he was still the big brother and he put me in my place when necessary. In every sense of the word, Chuckie was a big brother to me. While my parents worked, he made sure I was safe and cared for. Whether he liked it or not, Chuckie was my protector. He took a fair share of the switches and spankings that were meant for me. Chuckie dragged me around with him everywhere he went; I was constantly under his watchful eye. Chuckie was also my very first coach and mentor. He taught me how to play baseball and football- you name it! Being the first son carries a different set of responsibilities than being the second son. At a very tender age, Chuckie had to stand tall for me and I thank him graciously for that. I'll always appreciate and love him for the role he played in my life!

Family means everything to me. Family isn't always limited to blood relatives; family can also be non-relatives who are an extension of love and support. I can't say I remember it, but when my parents brought me home from the hospital, they hired a nanny to care for me: her name was Ms. Lula Thomas. Ms. Thomas was an older, God-fearing, southern, Black woman who never really talked much, but she always carried this little paperback book entitled, "The Daily Word" in her apron pocket. She read it every chance she got. Funny, how many years later, I found myself reading that same little book, and believe me, that continues to be a win for me. Ms. Thomas taught me the value of carrying the strength of God's word everywhere I went. Fresh home from the hospital, my parents handed me over to my nanny, Ms. Thomas. She took one look at me and said, "Wow, he's such a little peewee!" Ever since then, Peewee became my nickname. Imagine, being called Little Peewee... Sometimes I was called Peedle, Peety, WePee, any variation of Peewee folks could think of. It was awful and I never liked it, and at times, I was teased because of my nickname. Being called Peewee was sometimes hard to hear, but I learned a valuable life lesson behind it. I learned that when people impose challenges upon you, you have to rise above that challenge. Ms. Thomas gave me my first real challenge in life and I'd actually love to thank her and let her know I rose above that challenge and all that came with it, just like all of the other challenges I faced. Truly, that's the definition of winning! Ms. Thomas passed away many years ago, but she'll never be forgotten.

My parents, my brother and Ms. Thomas all played significant roles in shaping me to become the person that I am today and that's a major league win for me. Without their mentoring and sacrifices, I am certain that my life would have turned out very differently.

Young Army Lt Charles R. Collins before combat and Delois C. Collins well dressed Chicago socialite.

My father well after the War sporting his repaired face, out on the town with DeLois.

14

CHAPTER II
GETTING IN THE GAME

As a young boy, there were sights and sounds that I will always remember. Like the first time I went to Wrigley Field, home of the Chicago Cubs. What a site it was for me, an 8 year old boy. When I first heard the ball hit the bat, it was like nothing I'd ever heard in my field of dreams. The crack of that bat got my attention. This was the big leagues. You could smell the food as soon as you entered through the gates. For me, that made eating burgers and hotdogs synonymous with baseball. We only got a few opportunities to go to professional games, so that smell and those sounds were few and far between, until I met Mr. Thompson, my little league coach and my friend Squeaky's father. He took us to this place called "Fred and Jacks" located near 76th and Vincennes, after our little league games. Fred and Jack's had the absolute best freshly cut French fries, hot and salty, and you had your choice, of a burger or hotdog. I would always choose the burger, because I could always get a dog at home. Those burgers were greasy good, juice dripping down the side of your mouth with mustard, grilled onions, the works. Not to mention they had the best thick milkshakes in town. The challenge was which one to choose- strawberry, chocolate or vanilla? Fred and Jack's was one of those places where you could still taste the food long after eating it. We now had our place and we looked forward to going there. Fred and Jack's became motivation to play well, because if Mr. Thompson was hungry and we played well, he would take us there as a treat.

Squeaky and I became best friends. As teenagers, we double dated, went to senior prom, drive-in movies, all those things friends did together. To this day, we are still the best of friends, but we try to go by our real names now, Ed and Robert, which is challenging because people knew us as "Squeaky and Peewee." That friendship has lasted all of these years as we continue to talk on a regular basis. Most of my friends are from my old neighborhood and the team; we are still very close friends to this day. Great friends are tremendous wins!

Mr. Thompson was a World War II veteran with numerous awards for his courage and bravery, including an honorable Purple Heart. He was also my first professional mentor. Back in the day, he was the captain and quarterback of his high school football team at-DuSable High School. After high school, he was drafted into the Army, where he showed his leadership skills even in his early years.

Mr. Thompson's military training mimicked his coaching style- stern discipline; it was his way or the highway!

Looking back, his secret to winning was simple: master the basic fundamental skills of the game, coupled with rigorous-repetition, plus attention to detail, all while having fun. It worked and it kept our attention.

I took that philosophy with me through my years of coaching and I can honestly say, using his methods (along with others I learned along my journey) have afforded me a very successful coaching career. Mr. Thompson was consistent with our daily practice regiment. During the summer, we practiced every morning at 10am sharp. He gave us boys a heavy dose of his fundamentals: Mr. Thompson worked hard and he expected us to work hard too! After working his second job, he would go home around 7am and get a few hours of sleep before our practice. He didn't miss a beat. He had us on that field drilling us like soldiers. He was very serious in his training approach and committed to our excellence.

That experience taught me that how you present yourself is a reflection of your work ethic. It's important to show up strong, be well prepared and have the ability to sustain and execute under pressure. Another win I realized.

In order to provide his sons an opportunity to play on a team, Mr. Thompson began coaching Little League. He got a late start with the local park district, so the teams were already set. He had to take the kids that weren't chosen for a team that first year along with his own young son and form his own team. They won a few games in their first season, but lost most of the time. By this time, his competitive juices were aroused; he was naturally a winner. He instinctively knew how to win. Once he realized how the league worked, he went to work shaping our team. By now, we were-eleven years old and we had begun to win games by large margins. The league officials wanted to split up our team because we were that good. Mr. Thompson was determined not to allow that to happen, so we migrated to Abbott Park where we joined forces with some other teams and entered the city playoffs. It wasn't quite the same because the other boys didn't have that full training Mr. Thompson had provided to us, and as a result, we lost the city title that year. It was a crushing blow that brought me to tears. I didn't get a chance to play in the city playoffs and I could feel the hurt on Mr. Thompson. I knew we only had one year remaining left to play in the Little League and I was not going to let another victory slip away from us.

After that experience, we lost some key players and for some reason I took it upon myself to help put our team back together. That spring, my family and I moved out of the court way. I made new friends who knew how to play ball and they wanted to join our team. So, the following spring, I recruited Big Pete, Little G.T and Dwight to our team. All three of these boys became big time contributors. Years later, Mr. Thompson would call me his general manager because I had brought in the talent and he coached it! I was extremely proud the day he mentioned that amongst the now older team members.

For our last year in the Little League, we returned to Tuley Park and dominated the league, crushing our city rivals in the wake. Mr. Thompson always made sure we played our very best. One strategy he used was to pit us against our toughest competitors as a way of preparing us for the city playoffs.

On game day, the scene was 10 or 12 boys lined up on Mr. Thompson's front lawn, dressed in our white uniforms with royal blue trim. He was meticulous about having a clean uniform and if it wasn't, you got sent home. We all felt proud when we put on that uniform. Just the year before, we changed our team name from the Braves to the Comets. Mr. Thompson had us vote on our new name and pick our own jersey number and that made us feel a strong sense of pride and confidence in ourselves. We earned the right to proudly wear that uniform. I was also proud that I got my number preference; I got to wear number 1 on my back and many nights I fell asleep in my Comets' uniform.

As a young ball player, I was determined to be in the starting line-up. When the playoffs started and just before we loaded up the car to travel, Mr. Thompson would come out on his porch. With his pencil and pad in hand, he would sit down in his old metal lawn chair. That was my own mental que to run up alongside him and stand right near his shoulder. As he began to write down his starting lineup, I stood there anxiously waiting while he looked around at the others warming up. After what seemed a lifetime, he wrote down, R. Collins playing right field. The very first name on the line-up was me; I'm the lead-off man! I had struggled for a spot in the starting lineup, but one of our players fell from grace with Mr. Thompson- his lack of hustle and lackluster attitude got him demoted. I was now the next man in line and boy was I ready. I kept that pattern before every game and he kept writing "R Collins" and I just kept playing my butt off for that man. He had given me a chance and I was determined not to blow it.

At the early age of 12, I had no real strategy about how to get into the lineup, but I was always trying to be first in whatever the team did. Even if it was just a foot race, I was always one of the first. I knew I had to play hard, continue to get hits, play good defense- and that's all I thought about. I gave it 100%, was always on time, ready for practice and I know that is something Mr. Thompson expected from everyone. As I look back on things now, I realize that how I positioned myself with those traits served me well; I consider them winning strategies.

When we rode to the games, everyone rode in the same seat each time. Hey! We were winning and you can't change up patterns like that. I sat in the middle, up front next to Mr. Thompson everywhere we went. I felt we had a real special bond between us. We won the south section title, and I had played so well at that point that he gave me a new nickname, "The Mighty Mite." He continued to call me that until his dying days. I was proud of that nickname because it perfectly described my power and size. I was thrilled that he recognized that in me, and Mr. Thompson crowning me with that name made it even more special. He made me feel like a real winner.

During the playoff season, there was some racial tension within the surrounding neighborhoods. We had to go into park districts where there was a heavy police presence needed for a safe environment during the game. These neighborhoods had never seen an all-Black team. Boy, were we a sight to see! When we warmed up, we were flawless, and many teams were intimidated just by watching us. The semifinal game was probably our toughest opponent all summer. They were from Lindblom Park and they had an outstanding team with the very best pitcher we had faced all summer- Peter Quirk. Believe me, if you can still remember a player's name, then you knew he had to be good.

The game was extremely tight. Tension built with every pitch. It was the last inning. Game tied, 1:1. Both pitchers were dominating the game. Two outs and two batters ahead of me. Then suddenly, there was an unexpected walk. Man on base. Now I just needed one more guy to get on base. Palms sweating. Heart pounding. Everybody was pumped! We had a lucky bunt single. Two guys on base. The fans cheered wildly! All eyes on me; seemed like everyone was calling my name. " Let's go Peewee! C'mon man!" they screamed. Nerves rattling. I reached down to dry my sweating hands with dirt. When I looked up, I saw Mr. Thompson coaching third base. The bench and fans' cheers were growing louder and louder. My eyes locked with Mr. Thompson's eyes. His smile radiated his confidence in me. Above the noise he mouthed, *Let's go, Mighty Mite!*" Hands now dry, my butterflies settled down and I dug in to hit. That first pitch from Peter was a blazing fastball that I barely saw coming. Strike! Next pitch, a hanging curveball. I jumped on it! A hard line drive placed perfectly to left center cleared the bases. I was standing on third base with a triple. The crowd was on their feet going wild. I heard Mr. Thompson saying, *"Way da go, boy!"* Last inning, bottom of the 7th and 1,2,3, they fell like dominoes! Game over! Score 3-1.

Finally, we had now reached that last platform, a best of three series to decide the City Champion. The stage was set. The first game would take place at Tuley Park, our home field. World Series banners swayed proudly to and fro. This event had attracted family and neighborhood support. Wow, our dreams were coming true!

Last year we were defeated by Waveland Park and we looked forward to a rematch this year. As luck would have it, our rematch dreams were thwarted- Norwood Park defeated Waveland and they were now our new rival. We knew nothing about them. We just knew what we needed to do. Our mentor made us understand quickly, don't take anyone for granted; they're here for a reason.

We won that first game 2-1 as the big play came from my friend Squeaky, catching a hard line drive at third base, stopping their threat with the bases loaded. Solid defense and stellar pitching saved the day. The next day, we traveled to Norwood Park. With our goal within reach, we wasted no time. Mr. Thompson's last comment before we batted in that first inning was, *"Jump on 'em!"* a phrase he used quite often. And jump on them we did! We loaded the bases in the first inning and our big thumper and star pitcher, Pete Swain, did his thing.

A mammoth drive that cleared the bases! Before they could even bat an eye, we were up four to nothing. You could see the humiliation on their faces. Solo shots in the next four innings by Squeaky, Eddie, Big Luke and a second one by Pete. The deal was sealed! Bonus, Big Pete and Squeaky combined to throw a no-hitter. We had shown our coach with that 8-0 shut out exactly what he had expected from us, perfection! The Tuley Park Comets were City Champions!

Our final goal was to win the very prestigious Thillens Stadium Invitational Tournament that had eluded us in the past two years. This tournament featured teams in the Midwest where past winners moved on to the Little League World Series in Williamsport, PA.

With our steady hitting and superb pitching, we slaughtered some very good teams to get to the finals. Now, we faced a well established team in Lexon A. C. They were very good and well coached with a sterling lefty on the mound that baffled many of us. The big play that day came from our second baseman Little Dave Floyd. Late in the game, with Lexon threatening, Dave made an over-the-shoulder catch saving me embarrassment, as it was actually my play to make in right field.

That nail biter was a 3-2 victory! We won the Thillens Tournament, winning four pressure packed games, against the very best teams and making our final record 32-0 for the season. What an accomplishment!

Unfortunately, we never received an invitation to the World Series. We always wondered why we were overlooked, but it was during racially tense times, and I'm sure inviting an all-Black team was not a priority. Mr. Thompson reminded us that we had so much to be proud of and told us not to worry about adult oversight. I know he wasn't happy, but he never let it bother us. We learned from it.

Mr. Thompson had taught us valuable lessons along the way. I specifically remember one in humility. After defeating Peter Quirk's team, (he was the white star pitcher from Lindblom) his dad asked Mr. Thompson if Peter could practice with us and join our team for the Thillens Stadium Tournament. Mr. Thompson agreed and for the first time, we had a white boy on our team. The take-away for our team was that it's not about the color of your skin, it was about a young boy who wanted to play with winners. It took a lot of guts for Peter and his dad to approach Mr. Thompson, but once again, our coach and mentor was teaching us another valuable lesson in life: inclusion and humility.

Mr. Thompson put his heart and soul into that team, pushing us harder and harder to be the best. He knew we had the experience and desire to win that championship, and he carefully molded us together with many great life lessons of humility, work ethic, preparedness and competitiveness. He blended that with lots of love as well as ice cream, burgers and milkshakes all of which he liked as well, when we won a big game. Even in his toughness, he was a giving person along with his wonderful wife and our second mother, Mrs. Frieda Thompson. She was our first aid when we had accidents, gave us water when we were thirsty, and she always had some hotdogs for us to eat as we played tirelessly in their backyard. Their home was our home and our parents loved it; they knew the Thompson's and felt we were safe whenever we were there.

Mr. Thompson passed away in Aug. 2017. I'll always cherish the many moments we spent together; he will forever remain in my heart. Mrs. Thompson, is now 97 years young and very much alive and well. Many of the boys I played with still call and keep in touch with our second mother to this day. She was that special lady behind an incredible man, as they were married for nearly 70 years. That's a winning combination if I ever saw one. I was blessed with a win, the first day I met this family.

Sporting my Comets uniform with mom and brother as dad warmed up for the father son game at end of the season. Won That Too!

Peter Quirk, the best pitcher the Comets ever faced.

CHAPTER III
DIAMOND OF HEROES

On May 19th 1944, my grandma Murty received a Western Union telegram stating that her son, 2nd Lt. Charles R. Collins, was "missing in action." It was all too much for poor Grandma Murty's heart to bear- she fainted. The news of my dad missing sent shock waves throughout our family and community.....

WWII. May 17, 1944, 2nd Lt. Charles R. Collins led a patrol in Bougainville along with a contingent of men from the 93rd Cavalry Reconnaissance Troop-the only African American Division in the Pacific. Bougainville, located in the Solomon Islands, was a maze of swamps, rivers and rugged hills. The jungle vegetation was so thick and dense that it was nearly impossible for soldiers to determine who they were shooting at, much less, where shooting was coming from. As the men traversed across the difficult terrain, the stench of rotting animals and human carcasses filled their nostrils. Ambushed by superior enemy firepower and numbers, the battalion was pinned down for several days in a swamp where they were forced to hide out. Three troopers were immediately killed. Three others were critically wounded and barely ambulatory. Collins was the fourth wounded (Source: Warfare History Network). He survived being shot in the face and had shrapnel wounds to his arms and legs. His lower eyelid was torn off as the bullet went through his nose. As a result, Collins was temporarily blinded.

The remaining men withdrew, believing those left behind had been killed and their bodies unrecoverable. As it happens, Staff Sergeant Rothchild Webb collected all of the wounded, including Lieutenant Collins, whose moans and groans could be heard beneath the sounds of rapid gunfire. In an effort to distract the enemy, Webb dispersed a hand grenade and dove deep into the jungle to retrieve his lieutenant. Under Webb's guidance, the brave soldiers hid out for three days in heavily, enemy-infested surroundings until they reached their own base. Still under machine gun fire, Sgt. Webb was able to move his seriously injured and bloodied Lieutenant Collins into the dense undergrowth, while the enemy scoured the deep bushes for them. Later, Webb and Collins took shelter in a nearby swamp, where Sgt. Webb administered spiritual and physical aid. With no food or clean water in sight, the possibility of gangrene setting in became ominous. Distraught and fatigued, Sgt. Webb retrieved a tiny, gold-plated bible from Lieutenant

Collins. He flipped to Psalm 23 and began to read aloud: *"The Lord is my Shepherd; I shall not want. He maketh me to lie down in green pastures."* Collins joined in: *"He leadeth me beside the still waters. He restoreth my soul..."* Surrounded by swamp and gun fire, these two men activated their deep faith to deliver them from the bowels of a hellacious reality. The word of God says, *"Where two or three are gathered together in my name, I am there with them." Matthew 18:20*

Dazed and confused, Webb asked Collins," which direction should we travel in order to get back to our base?"

Collins replied, "Based on yesterday's calculations, we will travel east." Having given the order, Webb carried Collins for three days through enemy territory, all the while under the constant threat of both men potentially losing their lives.

Years later, Sargent Webb was awarded the Silver Star, for meritorious service-one of the highest awards ever given by the United States Army. Lieutenant Collins received the Purple Heart, the Oak Leaf Cluster and the Bronze Star for bravery under fire.

Unfortunately, my father faced many surgeries and a yearlong rehabilitation after his experience in Bougainville. Several months later, he completed his tour of duty as a spokesperson for plastic surgery; he traveled across the country to military bases speaking to soldiers about the pros and cons of plastics. His example taught me that-winners share their experiences, good and bad, so that others may win too. I was born just after the war, so I only knew my dad's face with his scars healed. I did uncover some graphic pictures of his face just after surgery and it literally took my breath away... Those scars told the story of my dad's tremendous courage and his healed face represented a new chapter in his life; a fresh beginning. Still, I knew him to be a handsome, strong man that I admired and was extremely proud of. He was a quiet motivator with unwavering faith. In tough times, winners remain steadfast in their faith.

During the war, Black soldiers created strong, lifelong bonds with other soldiers they met across the country. The same issues of segregation and racial discrimination back home in the United States was also apparent on the war battlegrounds of Europe, East Asia and the islands of the Pacific Ocean. Up and coming Blacks at that time like Joe Louis, heavyweight champion of the world and Jackie Robinson, Major League Baseball's first African American player, could be found in the Cavalry Replacement Training Center at Fort Riley Kansas. After basic training camp, Joe Louis, Jackie Robinson and my dad, respectively, were sent to Ft. Riley Kansas to join a Cavalry Unit. Upon arrival, Jackie Robinson and my father applied for Officer Candidate School (OCS). The Black applicants' inclusion into OCS was delayed. Off the record, they were told that Black soldiers simply lacked leadership skills. My father's application, however, was accepted, and he successfully completed OCS training. My guess is that Jackie Robinson, being a darker-skinned brother, presented a problem for the chief administrators of the OCS. Fair-skinned Blacks often got a pass in situations like this-my father was a fair skinned Black man. Makes me wonder, what they really thought of him....

Feeling unfairly treated by the delay, Jackie began to fight for civil rights for people of color. He got an assist from Joe Louis and Truman Gibson, assistant civilian aide to the Secretary of War. After strong, bigoted opposition, they won that battle and Jackie was reassigned to Fort Hood Texas where he joined the 761st "Black Panthers" Tanks Battalion. This intense, possibly life shattering experience, led to a strong bond and personal friendship between two proven winners: Joe Louis and Jackie Robinson.

Prior to enlisting in the Army, Joe Louis had made a name for himself as a gifted boxer. Favorably, he was asked to perform exhibition boxing matches to entertain the troops prior to being shipped off to Germany. Winning at the sport of boxing seemed to pay off for the "Brown Bomber." His career statistics of sixty-six victories and only three losses, placed him as one of the greatest boxers of all time. Joe trained diligently and worked extremely hard at his craft to become his very best. Over my tenure in coaching, diligence to your craft and a strong work ethic were values that I insisted on from the young people I coached. You might say that I passed down those skills as they were also demanded of me as an athlete.

Winning is not always about what you know, but it's often about who you know. Ted Smith can be credited as the person who introduced my father and Jackie Robinson to one another. My dad and Ted knew each other well before entering the Army. Ted was a baseball scout for the Negro League. He also shared a friendship with Jackie Robinson. Ted introduced Jackie to my father and the two became fast friends. Often, they spent time together breaking bread or just chatting each other up during their down time at basic training camp and the Officer Candidate School. As Jackie's Major League dreams began to take root, Ted's career also soared. He took a job as a scout for the Brooklyn Dodgers. This move allowed him to stay close to Jackie. When the Dodgers played in Chicago, Ted took Jackie under his wing- a much needed break from the stress of interacting with the racism he encountered. Another safe haven for Jackie Robinson was time well spent at the Collins' household.

One day while my brother and I were playing catch, a car turned into the court-way and pulled up to our front door. Out stepped, Uncle Ted and Jackie Robinson. I was mesmerized! I remember looking up to this big, very dark-complexioned man wearing a white shirt and tie, as if he were going to a five star restaurant. He flashed his pearly-white teeth with a warm, infectious smile. I couldn't take my eyes off of him. His skin was so beautifully dark it literally glistened on his cheeks and forehead, giving his skin a magical glow. While serving together in the army, my dad and Jackie had become close friends. Due to segregation and the pervasive racism experienced by Black people across the country, there were many spaces and places where Black folk simply were not allowed to occupy. Some restaurants on the north side of Chicago were white only dine-in places. Fortunately for me, that worked to my advantage. Both my mom and dad were excellent cooks, so when the Dodgers came to town, mom and dad invited Jackie to dine at our home. That night we feasted on sauced up, fall off-the-bone barbecue ribs and chicken, maple-flavored baked beans and mom's delicious homemade potato salad. A summer spread any hungry ball player would enjoy! Jackie enjoyed that meal so much he said it was the best meal he'd ever had on the road, and he looked forward to his next trip to Chicago. That was a day I would not soon forget.

After dinner, Jackie rolled up his sleeves and played catch with my brother and I. He surprised us with new baseballs that I truly wish I had preserved. Probably would have been worth some cash or at least great conversation today... Any ball we got back then we played with until it darn near disintegrated, and then we would tape it up for its last bit of life. As we played catch with Jackie, he said something to the effect of, "Hey Chuck, your boys are pretty good!" I was only 8 years old at the time, but I remember feeling encouraged and motivated by his words. I've always tried to encourage the young people that I've coached and mentored by keeping a positive word in their minds. Sometimes, a positive word just might be all someone needs to push forward. I've noticed that most winners adapt the habit of encouraging themselves as a way of also encouraging others. The time I spent daily playing catch with my dad and brother paid off! I was confident that Jackie Robinson recognized that I had some skills.

The day after Jackie's first visit, he invited us to the Dodgers vs. Cubs game. This would have been my second time visiting Wrigley Field, but the big difference was Jackie provided front row seats for us right next to the Dodgers' dugout. That's the day I became a Brooklyn Dodgers fan for life. What a treat to have the players come over and welcome us. Having the opportunity to meet Peewee Reese, Roy Campanella, Don Newcombe, Gil Hodges, Duke Snider, all Dodger legends, was a dream come true and an amazing memory that I will hold onto for life. That experience impacted my life in so many ways; it was an honor to witness the humble spirit of these men. In addition to being some of Major Leagues' baseball's best athletes, they were indeed a class act. They carried themselves as a team of real winners!

These two men have literally guided my life and thinking: Jackie's life struggles; breaking barriers to enter into the Major Leagues; and his fight against discrimination and for civil rights for people of color.

In contrast, my dad fought on the frontline battlefield of WWII and nearly lost his life. He activated his faith and trust in God to get through a harrowing moment, and every day, he leaned into his devotion and love for his family to keep himself and us cared for and covered. Of the many tokens of love my dad left for me, the one I cherish the most is the tiny pocket-sized, metal-faced bible that my dad carried with him on the Bougainville battlefield. To this day, it remains stained with dried blood- my dad's blood. That was nearly 80 years ago, a lifetime in passing... My dad carried that bible close to his heart and now I carry it close to mine as a reminder of the love we shared, his great courage under fire and his unmatchable winning spirit.

Every time I think times are tough and life seems unfair, I'm reminded about the dire situations both my father and Jackie Robinson endured and it gives me the motivation to fight through life's challenges like a real champ. What these two special men survived in those days was no easy feat; they demonstrated tremendous bravery and courage under fire during the toughest of circumstances. I consider myself blessed to have shared an intimate relationship with both of these modern-day heroes.

Jackie Robinson, with my dad and I. I will never forget that dinner!

CHAPTER IV
IT'S ALL ABOUT THE TEAM

Webster's Dictionary defines the term *leader* as a guide, a conductor; a person who has commanding authority or influence. I believe that a leader provides guidance and direction at every turn. As Deputy Director of Athletics at Northern Illinois University, a huge portion of my job was to develop and execute programs to best serve the student athletes during their challenges. Attending classes and studying coupled with the responsibility to their particular team sport could be overwhelming for many. My role was to teach the necessary life skills that would strengthen their possibilities of success in and after college. This was no easy task as I had to make them aware of the pitfalls in life- as many students were unaware of the ramifications that could cost them their careers. I began to present them with information about drugs and alcohol abuse, date rape, driving without proper credentials, gambling and many other unforeseen issues. Realizing these dangers, they began to analyze and recognize for themselves situations they should avoid.

Flashback. Summer of 1973. It was an early evening in the "nightclub district" of 87th & Stony Island. Lots of people milling about on the streets. Some brotha's were standing on the corner, trying to collect some coins. While others, like me, were headed to The Dating Game for some cool jazz and a nice drink. I looked up and low and behold, there he was, "Wash" (short for Washington)a young man I had coached many years ago. Our eyes locked momentarily before that familiar grin slowly spread across his face. *"Hey Coach Collins, you remember me?* He was surprised when I said, *"Yes, yes, I remember you,Wash."* He had aged a great deal and the strong odor of alcohol lingered like a dark cloud around him. Immediately becoming aware of himself, he mumbled an apology for his disheveled appearance and said, *"Man, I'll never forget the guidance and positive messages you taught us. I kinda went the wrong way, but I know we all appreciated what you tried to instill in us. Much love to you Coach Collins."*

In my quiet time, I've realized the value of an encouraging word. As a mentor, you don't fully know a young person's situation. But when we encourage and support with positive words, we are affirming the value of young people and giving audience to their future. For so many young people, they may not have good role-models in their everyday lives to show them what's possible for the future. Mentoring is modeling appropriate and expected behavior; it's showing young people how to properly carry and conduct themselves. It's giving them a blueprint for a life with promise and possibility. I've come to accept that not every young person will follow the blueprint... some young folks, like Wash, will march to the irregular beat of their own drum. It's been a long time since my encounter with Wash...I'm hopeful that he has forged a new path in life and found a more consistent drumbeat to follow.

Through mentoring, I have discovered that some students will indeed march to the beat of their own drum and under most circumstances, that is ok; life is all about discovering your passion and then living it! This was the case with a young man on the 8th grade basketball team I coached at Avalon School. His name was Alan King. He was quiet, yet appeared to be more mature than most kids his age. One day, Alan didn't show up for a big game. All during the game, I was concerned about his absence. After the game, I went in search of Alan. When I pulled up to the alley behind his home, he was out there with several older guys working on cars. Alan began to tell me of his real passion for cars and after our conversation, we both agreed he would pursue his passion and leave the team. I was happy for him because I could see that special glow that people have when they've found their dream.

I began to have discussions with young people about pursuing and preparing for the future, so I couldn't in all consciousness not encourage him to go for it. He appeared to be quite relieved; he thought he was letting me down. We embraced, and enjoyed the moment. Little did I know that would be our last conversation. A very short time later, Alan, only 14 years old, was killed in a tragic car accident along with three other young passengers. Details revealed that he was the driver and unfortunately, he crashed into a family of four, who were also killed. The car was reported traveling at a speed of over 100 miles per hour.

When I received the news, I was devastated. I immediately went to see my dad, who I knew would understand my feelings. As he consoled me he said, *"Son, you have a great ability to serve and support young people, but remember, you won't be able to save them all!"*

Since that time, in critical and possibly life changing discussions with young people, I try to go the extra mile and look deeper into their situation and conversations to ensure I've reached the depth of their issues. For a long time, I felt there had to be something else I could have said to save Alan, and the other precious young lives that were lost. Eventually, I determined that God's plans for each of us supersedes our own plans. We may not fully understand God's plans, but I yield to God that God knows all and God knows best.

As we mature, life provides us with many memorable experiences, some valuable and some dreadful. I've always shared with my myriad of student athletes and mentees, that life is full of ups and downs, yet the true test of one's character resides at the bottom of that curve. I would ask, do you have the resolve to pick yourself up when life has given you a real gut punch? Many people can't make the climb back and others look to cast blame elsewhere when in actuality, they may not have had the experience or know how. My role as a mentor was to reinforce and support the efforts of my mentees; to be that sturdy bridge for my mentees to cross. Some students may effortlessly sail across the bridge, confident and self-assured, while others may view the bridge with so much ambivalence that they are unable to move forward, rendering them stuck at a crossroad. Occasionally this is where winners are born, deep down in the belly of despair.

Coaching and mentoring students can come with unexpected challenges that can derail a student's progress if not addressed immediately. One huge challenge I faced comes to mind. I had just come out of a meeting with Dr. Jacquline Simmons, the principal at Paul Robeson High School, located in the very tough Englewood community on Chicago's south side. This particular meeting culminated with her offering me the head men's basketball position. I was very excited and extremely optimistic about that opportunity; the team and community had an abundance of basketball talent.

Before I got too excited, Dr. Simmons informed me of my first challenge that had to be met head on.

"Coach Collins, unfortunately one of your basketball players, Alfrederick Hughes, will have to be sidelined until his grades are up to par and you need to inform him of this."

I replied, *"I will handle that!"*

I left the meeting with Dr. Simmons having mixed emotions. I was not looking forward to meeting with Alfrederick for two reasons: for one, he and I didn't know each other, so I wasn't sure how he would react to the news. Second, being that he was arguably the best player in the Public League, a situation of this sort would likely bring about public ridicule for Al and bad press for Robeson High School, neither of which we needed.

As fate would have it, minutes later, I ran into Alfrederick in the hallway, introduced myself and asked if he had a minute to talk. Al stood about 6'4 inches tall and weighed a good 200 pounds. Physically, he was a very intimidating figure. I, on the other hand, stood 5 foot 9 inches tall and weighed much less. The moment of truth was before us as we stood face-to-face.

I had watched Al play during the summer, so I briefly tried to share some performance pleasantries before dropping the bombshell. After an exchange of another few words, I finally stammered,

"Al, unfortunately you won't be able to practice or play with the team until your grades improve. "

He was stunned and overwhelmed all at once. I could see his blood beginning to boil. The look on his face said, *who the hell is this guy telling me I can't play?* I gulped, then took a deep breath. My thoughts began to race. I didn't know this dude well enough to anticipate how he might react. I felt like he might punch me in the face. As we stood face-to-face in the middle of the school hallway, it was like we were frozen in time. All of the usual surrounding chatter came to an abrupt halt. No bells ringing to signal the change of classes. No cluster of students' laughter filling the air. No sound of locker doors slamming. Just. Total. Silence.

CHAPTER V
JUST WIN, BABY!

Growing up, winning was everything. Pickup basketball games. Touch football on Sunday mornings. Even pitching pennies. Just win baby, that was the goal. High school sports were no different, and competition drove me. Suddenly, it dawned on me that I haven't won them all, but my attitude going in was to always win! That meant giving it all I had. Every. Single. Time. The young people call it swag now. We were old school; we just played with a cool confidence.

When I attended Tennessee State University, I was with winners at the highest level. The TSU football team was 33-1-1 my first three years there. I witnessed the best college football team of that era. They had numerous first round draft picks each year, including recently inducted NFL Hall of Famer, Claude Humphrey.

During this fabulous period, there were zero Black football players in the (SEC)Southeastern Conference. Kentucky's Nate Northington entered in Sept 1967, and became the conference's first African American player. That meant, the majority of African American talent was in abundance at TSU, Grambling, Southern, Florida A&M and other Historically Black Colleges & Universities. Prior to my arrival, the basketball team had won the NAIA National Championship three years in a row. Legendary coach and mentor John B. McLendon was at the helm and led that historical charge. Another amazing team to observe were the world renowned Tennessee State Tigerbelles Women's Track team. Olympians Wilma Rudolph, Wyomia Tyus, and Estelle Baskerville were a few of the notable unbelievable winners. I got to know these winners, through classes, eating together in the dining hall and of course, parties. I had the opportunity to watch these winners train, prepare and receive unbelievable coaching. Their coaches happened to be my class professors in the Health and Physical Education Department where I pursued my degree. Even though I had no idea I'd end up coaching, obviously this experience allowed me to develop and perfect my craft. They knew how to win; they excelled in shaping and grooming winners.

I was in awe of these athletes; I admired their drive and determination. As we entered baseball season that spring, my star began to shine bright. They took notice when I led the team in hitting for the better part of my freshman season. Starting as a freshman was more of a big deal than I thought. My status drew attention in the school news, with my professors and also with the ladies. That was cool!

In reality, I was in the right place at the right time; I was amongst winners striving for perfection and excellence. I truly loved that experience. TSU created an amazing winning environment. I learned that a winning environment was a huge part of building a solid program. Get everyone moving in the same direction, with the same goals and believe in one another. That's key!

I truly believe I graduated because I had to balance performing in the classroom and on the field. Many people I knew fell victim to too much partying and ended up "rolling out"; they left school without completing. I was focused on maintaining my physical health and condition so that I was always ready to perform at my best. Don't get me wrong, I partied with the best of them! The Tigerbelles and my homies loved to party. But I always adhered to the athletic curfew and made sure I was ready for the next day's workout or game. I learned how to balance it all. I was learning to spell win.

My coaches and professors were great mentors. They always had an encouraging word coupled with motivation to inspire. I remember TSU legendary football coach Big John Merrit. He caught me in the hallowed halls of Keans Little Garden one day, where many of my classes and coaches' offices were located. Southern drawl in check, he chomped on his thick and ever present cigar, as he said, " *Son, you played a great game yesterday. You're gonna be a real winner. Work hard, baby!*"

He called everybody baby.

I replied, "*Thanks coach! I didn't know you were there.*"

"I wasn't, he said. *Word gets around!"*

Over time, I realized that one of the keys to building a winning program is the use of team motivation; everyone motivates each other. Coach Merritt's words to me were more than motivation; his words really boosted my confidence and self esteem. He made me feel important and valued. The coaches really wanted to see all of our teams win. Take notice my mentors, spread your ability to everyone you can touch. Cast your net wide. Your words have the ability to make an unimaginable and lasting impact upon those that you mentor.

As I maneuvered through these growing phases of college life filled with experts and caring adults, I was absorbing the finer points of building trust, care and motivation. The fundamental keys of having a positive approach and trusted knowledge had become my core. It's all about trusting that you know what you know. A prime example of this was the day when I fell off of my square.

Every athlete remembers their worst game played. I am no exception. We were playing our cross town rival Vanderbilt- a game we looked forward to each year. They were an all-white team and felt they were superior to us. This particular game was a real tense battle. We were nursing a one run lead late in the game. Eighth inning, 2-on-2-out and victory was in sight. Then, the unthinkable happened. Hard line drive hit to my left. Actually, it was a play I made routinely. The ball began to rise when I thought it was sinking. And as I tried to make a basket catch beneath my waist, the ball handcuffed me; it hit the heel of my glove and bounced away. Our opponents scored two insurmountable runs as we went down one, two, three in the ninth! After the game, Coach Whit put his arm around me and said. *"I don't ever have to worry about seeing that again. You're too good, shake it off. We got more games to play!"* I was speechless, but he let me know his confidence in me had not wavered. I was really down, truly embarrassed and highly disappointed in myself. The next morning, Coach Martin, who was one of my professors and the head basketball coach came to find me.

Coach Martin, a tall and very athletic man, was a former Negro League pitcher. Often, he would come to our workouts and throw batting practice from time to time. He loved baseball and attended most home games to support us.

I had gone to breakfast early so I could avoid my friends and teammates. I was feeling defeated, almost to the point of questioning my abilities. Coach Martin sensed my sunken spirit and said, *"Bobby get that head up and put that game behind you. Everybody makes mistakes, but now your test begins!"* He then used a basketball metaphor, *"It's time to rebound son, the true test of your ability and character lies ahead."* I had no response. I just nodded my heavy head. He then said, *"You guys start a road trip tomorrow. I expect your best effort."*

Early the next day while loading the bus, I could feel my teammates were not happy with me. The long bus ride to Huntsville, Alabama was extremely quiet. All I could think about was Coach Martin's efforts to get me back on track.

47

I thought to myself, he never comes to early breakfast. I determined he had come *just to lift me up!* More than ever, I was determined not to let him down. That moment, I realized I had a mentor in Coach Martin. He genuinely cared about my well-being.

The following day, we had an early game and I was both excited and anxious for the opportunity to redeem myself. Seconds after the umpire hollered, *"Play Ball!"*, I hit the first pitch of the game and probably the longest home run I had ever hit. My frustrations sailed right over that fence with the ball! By the end of the day, I had four hits and two great catches in centerfield. The icing on the cake was winning that game. I hit my stride; I regained my confidence. I was back, and I really owed it all to Coach Martin. The way he cared for me demonstrated to me what it meant to be a mentor.

When it comes to mentoring young people, timing is everything. Be observant and don't miss the moment. Later, as I recounted Coach Martin's technique, I took note of his impeccable timing. In that scenario, he moved with a sense of urgency to help me reset myself. Had he missed that moment, I may have fallen deep into a hole of self-pity and doubt.

We need more Coach Martins in the world; people who genuinely care about people. As you can see, mentors are extremely valuable and necessary as our roads and travels can become bumpy. Being there for someone in their time of uncertainty can be life saving. My moment was just a game, but it meant the world to me!

Then, it happened. That magical day, a day that changed my life and name forever.... It came.

CHAPTER VI
THEY CALL ME COACH

Those three boys. Those three young boys, on that first day of school at Avalon Elementary. Unexpectedly, they crowned me Coach. It was actually the first time I had ever been called *Coach*. I was feeling myself- as the young people say nowadays. "Coach"pretty much did it for me. I was all in, and I can't remember if I've ever looked back. In my excitement, I went home that night and began to prepare a practice plan for my students. My years of teaching in the classroom well prepared me for this next leg of my journey. I began to line up my coaching strategy: develop players through the use of fundamentals; demand team play; make it enjoyable!

Rigorous classes taught by experienced professors and coaches had also prepared me well. I was ready to lean into the mountains of coaching instruction I had received and apply it accordingly. At times, some folks frown upon the concept of coaching classes because they don't regard it as academic learning. This was not the case at TSU. The classes I took were college accredited and used a scientific modality. These programs were uniquely crafted and we were expected to learn and apply the techniques with our students. Our program administrators didn't want us to just be coaches, they wanted us to be experts in our field.

They Call Me Coach, was actually a book written by John Wooden, an athlete, author and arguably the greatest college basketball coach of all-time. Coach Wooden earned that title by mentoring, and guiding his mentees. He is credited with creating the famous *Pyramid to Success*, a diagram that boasts 25 common characteristics and traits to succeed at sports and in life. Skill, Conditioning, Self- Control, Team Spirit, Poise and Confidence are a few of the characteristics named on the pyramid. Wooden not only coached, but he taught the game of life through basketball. This method generally can sustain young people for a lifetime if administered with expertise, love and passion.

Personally, I am extremely protective of the title *Coach*. In my humble opinion, the title Coach is applied relatively free of challenge. Not everyone is equipped nor called to be a coach. Coaching is a calling; it's not a profession that you choose, it chooses you. Coaching is *heart-work*; it requires that you engage your heart. It's an awesome responsibility to mold, shape, influence and inspire the lives of young people. If you are blessed enough to coach, prepare yourself. There's a plethora of books on the market to help prepare most novices. No matter your age or experience, coaching requires careful planning and selflessness. You will be building character, life skills and young lives.

Having played for the Chicago Public Schools, the opportunity to coach was surreal. I understood the dynamics and history of CPS. It's competitive nature warmed my juices even more. After playing baseball mostly in my younger days, my interests shifted. I jumped at the chance to coach basketball in the public league. A very good friend of mine, Johnnie Butler, offered me a freshman/sophomore job. After the first year, I was promoted to head coach once Johnnie left for a college coaching position.

I was now in my element, with the opportunity to win! I took my leadership role quite seriously, vowing to not only teach basketball, but also to mentor the young people I would serve. For the next eight years, I was the head basketball coach. You might say that I was obsessed with those same feelings of, *Just Win baby, just win!*

After a brief stint at Calumet High School, I was blessed to land the head coaching position at Robeson High. You could say it was my dream job. They had talent, a great administrative leadership team and the support I needed. I was really beginning to feel, *this is how you spell win*; I was on top of the world. And then, my world came to an abrupt halt when I was met with one of the most challenging moments of my career. Recall if you will Alfredrick Hughes. When last we met, Alfredrick and I were at an impasse; Alfredrick was sidelined due to poor grades. I had just lowered the boom on

his aspirations to start as the power forward for the Robeson
Raiders and he was less than happy with that news. In fact, he
was downright angry! We were face-to-face, as his muscle-clad
frame towered menacingly above me. My heart was pounding
loudly in my chest and my thoughts were racing. I thought he
might punch me in the face. Trying to compose myself, I drew
in a deep breath and said,

 "*I'll help you and we will get through this together.*" Alfredrick said
nothing.

 He walked away pretty upset. Years later, he told me that he
hated my guts at that moment! I could definitely understand
where he was coming from. He faced the threat of public
ridicule because his anticipated stardom would soon begin to
fade away. It was going to require some very careful plans to
ensure that he could get back on track.

 Alfredrick didn't want to talk to anyone for a few days. After
giving him the space he needed, Principal Simmons developed
a team of what I would call, "angels"who would have the task
of making sure this young man reached his goals. A team of
compassionate, caring and experienced educators, counselors
and mentors and myself, designed a program to meet his needs.
Each of us were assigned a specific role to work with Al. I will
forever admire the commitment and dedication displayed by
Al's angel team. Everyone worked tirelessly to save this young
man from total despair and disappointment. Tutors, night
classes and extra work was assigned in order for him to catch
up. Equally important was the one-on-one time spent daily

nurturing Alfredrick's mind and spirit to keep him focused and motivated- not an easy task. As they said back in the day, "it takes a village to raise a child", and the" villagers" had taken this task to heart. Motivating and encouraging Al wasn't a cake walk- I simply hadn't gained his trust. It took some time for him to trust and accept that I was there to help him succeed. For me, it wasn't totally about basketball, it was about helping this young man regain his confidence and self-esteem so that he could ultimately achieve his dreams. Alfredrick had big dreams. He was that good; he had the potential to play at a high level in college, and probably play professional ball.

At that point, I began to negotiate with his emotions. I promised Al once he bought into the process we had laid out for him and he was thoroughly immersed in his own recovery, he could come to practice with the anticipation of playing again. Finally, after many long weeks of waiting, and what I considered my most challenging mentoring efforts, slowly but surely, Alfredrick began to change. He got on board with the academic plan and we began to see the fruits of his labor. As time began to tick in his favor, his day to return was within sight. At that juncture, I felt it was time for him to re-join the team. I wanted to motivate and encourage him even more, so a few weeks before his return, I allowed him to practice with the team. Unfortunately, I discovered he wasn't quite ready.

His first practice was rough! He was so vicious and aggressive toward his teammates- pushing, elbowing, trash talking etc, that I had to stop practice and inform him, *"You will not take out your frustrations on this team. And if necessary, we will play the entire season without you. We are a team!"*

There was no other stance for me to take- he left me no alternative. I just couldn't afford to lose the confidence of the other team members. Only the leader can close those gaps and I knew his teammates were watching.

Once again, that angry scowl appeared on his face. His expression said, who is this guy telling me what I can and cannot do - again! I couldn't sacrifice the entire team for one player. Alfredrick had to determine for himself if he was all in with the team or not.

I sent him home for the weekend to marinate in that message. I had no way of knowing if he would even return; he was just that angry! Much to my delight, not only did he return, but he apologized to me for his selfish actions and said he was ready to be a solid teammate.

A humble spirit will take you very far in life. Alfredrick had turned a corner. With a fresh attitude and his grades up to par, Al's self-esteem rebounded. My final comment to him at that moment was, *"Don't ever lose that aggressive and dominant attitude, but direct it toward our opponents."*

Moving forward, Alfredrick dominated every opponent we faced; he was a force to be reckoned with and other city schools began to take notice of him. His contributions to the team were immeasurable. The squad up to that point had actually played very well, and his addition made us a strong contender for the city crown!

For me, I realized once again, that winning wasn't about the trophy that eluded us, but the journey from adversity to success that helped transform a boy into a man. That's how I spell win! Alfrederick Hughes graduated from Robeson High and went on to play basketball at Loyola University of Chicago, where he became their all time leading scorer and the fourteenth pick in the NBA draft.

I had great teams at Robeson High School and for six years, we were extremely successful and highly respected. I made sure my teams looked good, played well and were highly competitive. Academic success and good citizenship were cornerstones of the program. I received compliments from principals and administrators from schools we visited. Our solid character combined with stellar play and sportsmanship drew attention. We would kick your butt with class. We won our conference a few times and played in the state super sectional. Even ranked number one in the Chicago area to start the 1983-84 season.

The wins came in abundance through solid relationships garnered while coaching. More rewarding than any trophy I've ever been awarded was the opportunity to bear witness to young people chasing their dreams and knowing that I had a hand in molding a dreamcatcher.

Sports is a win-lose situation, that's why you must determine early on how you spell win. Set the atmosphere for winning so that your mentees come to accept that winning, be it on the field or off the field, comes naturally. Adversity is a good teacher; not all wins come easily, but most come with a lesson that can be applied to life. These lessons build character and integrity, values that will carry young people far in life.

CHAPTER VII
BASES ARE LOADED

Sometimes, life just doesn't let you know where it will take you. That's why we must continue to grow. Be as ready as we can for any conversion or adversity that comes our way. At one point, I felt coaching high school basketball was my calling, but it wasn't my life forever. My Lord and Savior, Jesus Christ, had other plans for me...

I had begun to feel a little uncomfortable with the leadership in the public school system, specifically in athletics. Unfairness, corruption and favoritism became the norm and that was disturbing to me. Rules for the upcoming season were being established by the sports' administration, without coaches input and sometimes even mid-season. For example, coaches couldn't stand on the sideline during play. Preposterous! That cramped many coaches' style as kids many times learned through visuals. Unscrupulous coaches were offering students gifts and special favors to transfer. Game officials' assignments were done arbitrarily instead of via a merit system. This invited corruption to what I felt should have been a squeaky clean operation for our student athletes. It was important to me that honesty and integrity were values modeled not just by coaches and mentors, but also from the very institution we were representing. Young people need to see things done the right way. Even then, I was fighting to make things right. After all, I was a product of this very system. All of the mayhem began to weigh heavily on my spirit. Winning state titles for the public league became the administration's only desire and obsession. They had forgotten all about the true essence of winning: strategy, hard work, honor and integrity. Winning begins with a positive attitude and requires that you bring heart and soul to the playing field, court or whatever arena you're playing on. Cheating is never a good look; cheaters never win- not in the long run. Continued corruption eventually led to the erosion of many neighborhood programs. I had seen far too many kids being used for adult gratification, and it was sickening to me. In spite of many conversations and complaints, it appeared this would be the new norm. I couldn't, in my way of thinking, win that way.

Then came the call. The kind of call that requires a gigantic decision. Early, one midsummer morning, Jim Rosborough unexpectedly rang my phone. Jim was an assistant coach at the University of Iowa. He and I had met at the University of Iowa summer camp he directed and we had developed a friendly relationship. Jim had also coached and taught physical education in the Chicago Public Schools -an experience we had in common.

Saturday. 6:30am, my phone rang. Before I could even wonder why Jim was calling me at that god-forsaken hour, he blurted out,

"Robert, I'm going to be named head basketball coach at Northern Illinois University on Monday and I want you on my staff."

My thoughts went into a dozen different directions as he began to sell me on the idea. The perks. The growth opportunity. And of course, the chance to coach. It was all very attractive. After a few questions, I asked,

"When do you need an answer?"

"Later today would be great." he replied

"Give me a call this afternoon. I'll let you know." I said.

I probably sounded as if I had it all together. Clearly, I didn't. Anxiety and excitement flooded my body. I wasn't sure if I could make a decision in a week, let alone a few hours! I sat in silence for a few moments, reflecting. It was now about 6:45 am. A life changing call in 15 minutes. Very quickly, I began to weigh my options; I was leaning towards making the move. Generally, teachers continue teaching until retirement. That wasn't for me, it just wasn't. I felt there was a greater calling on my life and this opportunity was more in alignment with my purpose. I had several things at the top of my list I needed to evaluate before I could finalize my decision. My innermost thoughts were racing, but the care of my loved ones was most heavy on my heart. After steadying my emotions, I focused my thoughts and energy on my parents.

At that time, my dad was not in good health and he needed assistance with his day-to-day care. I lived a few short blocks away, so helping my mom with my dad's care was not an issue. I pondered if it was the right time for me to leave -maybe I can't do this now? My brother was nearby as well, but would I be leaving the burden of care on him? That hardly seemed fair. I was now tormented with the thought of leaving my dad when he needed me most.

As these and other thoughts raced through my head, I finally got dressed and went to see my dad. He was my dad, but also my first mentor. Why not just listen to his thoughts? After some small talk, and a little anxiety on my part, I told my dad about the call; I explained that I had some decisions to make. He stopped me right there. *"What decisions? This seems perfect for you"* he said.

Pause.. My voice began to crack.

"Dad, I'm concerned about you and I'm not sure this would be a good time to move away." I said.

Without hesitation he said, *"Son, I will absolutely die right now if I thought I was keeping you from your dreams! Your mom and I will be fine. You're not going to the moon. Go for it!"*

Wow! Didn't expect that response. Even in his weakness, my dad showed remarkable strength. Once again, the mentor in him showed up; he was coaching me from his side line, cheering me on to my own victory. While my heart swelled with love for the great courage he displayed,I knew that he was not fine. There were health challenges looming ahead for both my mom and my dad. The care for my father was still a big question. I couldn't just leave thinking that everything would work out. I needed to implement a plan of care.

In every person's life, there will be times of great sacrifice. It was incumbent on me to make critical decisions for the health and well-being of my parents. I've learned to look at the big picture, not just the polaroid of myself. It was the right thing to do. My parents were my world and I had to have a plan that ensured their comfort as well as mine. My upbringing made this decision very tough. My parents wanted me to be my own man. My dad never pushed me into the family business because he wanted me to find my own path. My dad believed that me finding my own way was my way to win. He was right when he said I wasn't going to the moon. Actually, I was only moving about 75 miles away- still close enough to assist physically and emotionally. That compromise was a win for me and it all began with my first mentor's encouraging words, "Go for it, son!"

Becoming my dad's caregiver was a pivotal point in my life. Where caregiving is concerned, I discovered that one day you will either need it or need to provide it. For me, the time had come for me to step up for my dad. I needed assurance that he would be fine and it was my responsibility to ensure his well-being; I had to make it work.

Having now gone through that situation, I have always admired those (and there are many) who sacrifice themselves in order to give much needed care to others. Caregiving is the most loving and kind act you can offer. As they say, experience is the best teacher. I found this to be true when caring for my dad. One morning, my mother called with real concern in her voice. She really wasn't trying to alarm me, but I quickly heard the distress in her voice and I immediately knew something was wrong. My dad needed a bath and my mom needed help bathing him. I immediately went to the house to assist. When I arrived, my dad was in the tub and unable to get out; he had no strength to lend in the effort. My mom weighed about 120 pounds and my dad about 180. At that time, I was about 165 pounds and in great shape. I figured my dad and I could negotiate this move from tub to bed, no problem. I had my mom step aside as I confidently took over the task. Needless to say, I was embarrassingly wrong. I never realized that due to my dad's declining muscles, his body was now dead weight; he could provide zero assistance. I had to lift him from the most awkward of positions. It was nearly impossible. Water splashing, slipperiness, the small space in which to work... After a good while struggling through this task, somehow or another, and I do mean somehow, we got him out of the tub and into bed. Suddenly, I concluded, my mother and I were not qualified to suitably care for him. Even though we both loved him dearly, I quickly realized he deserved better care than we could provide. Before my mom and I could even begin the conversation about dad's future care, my dad asked to speak to me alone. He asked me to come close so my mom wouldn't hear. In his weakening voice he said, *"Son, take me back to the VA (veterans hospital)."* My mom had just rented a new hospital bed for the home, thinking this is where he should be. He whispered, *"When you die while in the VA, the benefits differ from when you die at home.* That statement somewhat stunned me. *"I don't want my health to take its toll on your mother. Take me back!"*

He knew mom wanted him at home, but he also wanted her burden to be light. As usual, dad was selfless. I convinced mom this was the right thing to do. She didn't resist, as we both understood he needed professional caregiving.

Returning dad to the VA Hospital was the right move; he was provided with excellent care. Caregivers are such a true blessing and don't always come in the form of nurses or doctors, just compassionate, selfless people. We were assured by the staff that this war hero would get the very best of care.

Watching my parents age, I found myself leaning in a little deeper with the lessons and wisdom they had to share. I recalled the many times my father comforted grieving families through our funeral business. He always treated them with dignity and respect. Witnessing death himself up close and personal during the war, and now late in his tenured life, he understood the essence of those moments. In the end, I was at peace that I was able to offer the same compassion and respect to my parents.

CHAPTER VIII
SLIDING INTO HOME

To have and to hold the care of another human being in the palm of your hands is an awesome responsibility. Former President Barack Obama is quoted as saying, *"We are reminded that, in the fleeting time we have on this Earth, what matters is not wealth, or status, or power, or fame but rather how well we have loved and what small part we have played in making the lives of other people better."* Caring intimately for my dad taught me a lot about caring for the young people I mentored. I like to believe that for as much as my father enriched my life with the knowledge and wisdom he passed on to me, that I was able to pass on what I inherited from my father to my mentees. Everything I've learned from my dad, through trial and error and the life he lived, I believe, has made me a better man, a better father, a better mentor, coach and an overall, better human being.

I had made a very important decision to leave my coaching position at Paul Robeson High School and accept the new position of Assistant Basketball Coach at NIU. Telling my team of young athletes was the final step before my transition. I felt I had prepared my squads for challenges, but explaining my departure at this juncture would still be very difficult. Walking into the locker room, they were all smiles. We traded small talk. Guilt was penetrating my thoughts. I bounced back and forth between telling them and not telling them. Maybe this wasn't a good time to tell them after all? I had to be rational; I simply couldn't avoid the moment any longer. As I opened my mouth to speak, my voice slowly began to crack. I was breaking down before I could open up to them.

"Coach, what's up? You okay?" one of my players asked.

Without stalling any further I simply said, *"I'm going to be leaving fellas!"* The room got quiet momentarily. Then, suddenly there were questions and comments coming from everywhere.

"What do you mean, Coach?"

Why?"

"Is your dad okay?" They knew he was sick. After several more questions, one young man lightened the mood with a funny question,

"Did you get fired?" We all kinda chuckled at that.

That light-hearted moment opened the door for me to say, *"Gentlemen, I've taken a college job at NIU."*

Boom! There it was, out on the table. No turning back now! One of my more mature seniors offered,

"Congratulations coach! That's a good thing for you, right?"

Several of the others began to tear up;they were obviously upset.

"Not fair Coach!"

"What about us?" cried the underclassman.

"What about the season?"

"Who will coach us?"

"How can you leave now?"

With many of these questions out in the open, the room became hushed again, waiting for my answers. I really had to gather myself. I could never have anticipated this was going to be as emotional and trying as it was.

I responded, *"Gentlemen, this was a very tough decision for me. There comes a time when everyone has to make decisions. I have loved and treated you like my own and we will be forever bonded."* I reminded them that for the last eight years, seniors have waved goodbye to me. It was my turn to graduate and step into my future. I explained the need to follow my own dreams and opportunities. Still, I observed much confusion and uncertainty on their faces. It was clear that my words were not resonating with them and I needed to provide more clarity, so I dug deep into my soul, *"Gentlemen, follow your dreams. On your journey, you will discover that some doors may be closed to you. Kick down those doors and when you open them, reach back for another brother to come through. Take advantage of opportunities that have been offered to you, but also be mindful that you have the power to create your own opportunities. I hope to leave you in good hands with someone who will continue to assist you in thriving and striving towards your future. Be faithful! Always remain true to yourself and your craft."*

One by one, we hugged, high fived and shared our innermost

feelings with one another. Finally, that unsettling feeling drifted away. I knew that my team and I had the closure that we desperately needed.

It's important for young men to have positive, supportive, nurturing relationships with other men, especially if their father or father-figure is absent in their life. Young men need to see strong, positive models of what they can become and what the future holds for them. When a father, uncle, or brother is absent in a young man's life, reliable, consistent male mentorship is as good as it gets. The youth of today need direction. A good mentor can provide direction along with wisdom and love. I hesitate to think where I would be had I not had a supportive and caring father. He actually played both roles during my life, vacillating between being my father and being my mentor. As a young boy, there was always love in my heart for my dad. Yet in the back of my mind, there was also a little fear. My smart mouth, as my mom called it, was trouble and not doing what I was told would lead to consequences that my dad was assigned to handle. Back in the day, we received spankings or whoopings, as they say as punishment for misbehaving. Spankings were simply my father's form of discipline that had to be administered when I got out of line. Some spankings even came with the comment, *"Son, this is going to hurt me worse than it will hurt you!"* At the time, I'm not sure I bought into that, but I now realize that was probably true. Correction was love. My father hated the pain and tears that came as a result of a spanking; it hurt him to have to spank me. But as a parent, he felt that this was the best way to correct unacceptable behavior. A parent's love runs deep, very deep. I later came to realize that disappointment in my foolish choices was what my father felt, more so than anger. At some point, those spankings ceased, and in their place were talking sessions or designated time alone in my room to reflect on my behavior or choices. That reflection time is now referred to as "time out." A day, a week, whatever it took for you to get that message. Once those methods ran their course, I think that was when my dad shifted from being my father to becoming more of a mentor. I no longer feared spankings; I had matured and learned to carefully think things through and learn from my youthful mistakes. My dad gave me mental tools, so I could make better decisions. My parents were a stable, nurturing foundation for me; they were roots. But they also prepared me for independence; they instilled within me self-confidence, self-preservation and life- skills needed to succeed in the world. Their love and guidance enabled me to take flight and soar on my own.

Parenting and mentoring are two very distinct roles, and those distinctions must always be acknowledged and respected. Parenting is a life-long commitment to the growth, development and well-being of your child. As we raise our children, we also take into consideration how we were reared, being mindful to maintain those practices that compliment our individual parenting style while eliminating those practices that do not align with our own beliefs and values. On the other hand, the mentor relationship is focused on guiding, motivating, offering emotional support and modeling appropriate and expected behavior for the mentee. Mentors often share with their mentees snippets of their own career and life experiences as a way for mentees to gain perspective and begin to shape their own life. A mentor is water to a seed that has already been planted; mentors support the growth process of a young person.

Like my dad, I was blessed with the opportunity to be both a parent and a mentor. Being a parent changed many things in my life. My thinking and priorities were centered around my children. I absolutely loved the responsibility of parenting and quickly realized my image had to be one of discipline and solid character. I always wanted to project a positive image in their minds, by making sound decisions. Although I obviously made mistakes, I strived for perfection,always conscious of what they might see or think. Bearing that self-imposed weight, I believe, made me a better parent, for in their precious eyes, I was their champion. I parented with the love that was instilled in me. My grandmother would often refer to our clan as her "love army." Finally, after years of guidance and love, I recognized in the eyes of my own grown children, their love and approval for the manner in which they were parented.

Mentoring matured me personally as well. Through the experience of being a mentor, I acquired the skills of active listening. I had no problem in sharing my own personal stories, I had to learn how to listen from the heart for what they were sharing. I realized that active listening leads to deeper understanding. Spend some time, listen to their issues and dreams, encourage greatness, take them places they have never been before, mentally as well as physically. The ability to capture their story,the essence of who they are becoming, this is the main ingredient for planning strategies and effectively guiding young people to their best future. Once you have mastered this principle, the rewards of mentoring are priceless. Helping young people has always brought me great satisfaction, which is why I have such a loving passion for mentoring.

My most effective way of sharing the importance of sound decision making with my mentees was by offering up some of the mistakes I had made in my own life. I was comfortable letting mentees know I had made my fair share of mistakes. I felt they needed to know it's okay to confess blunders when they occur. My story of purchasing my first automobile was one I enjoyed sharing and had fun telling to my mentees.

Peering back, I had just turned 24 years old. I was working my very first professional job making enough to afford my own apartment, and pay a car note. I could still get a good meal from mom, so I saved a little there. I was feeling independent and confident, so after saving about two thousand bucks, getting that first car became my main priority. I had dreamed of that day and had very high hopes and expectations. I was a young adult at this point, yet still inexperienced in decisions of this magnitude. Thinking I was prepared to make a good purchase because I had money, was a costly mistake. I can still see that car. It was a brownish-gold color; it looked good on the showroom floor, but once I took the car outside, it was an ugly, plain brown. Yuk! I couldn't believe I bought a brown car. It was an odd shaped Subaru and after a day or so, it appeared to be much smaller than I thought. Shaking my head...What had I done?

A week after the purchase I became totally dissatisfied with the car- it simply wasn't what I wanted. The color, size, even the look, just wasn't right. Clearly, I had made a mistake. Now I had a problem that couldn't be corrected. Immediately, I had to learn from this snafu.

What I took away from that experience was that you must do your homework before making decisions. The car dealer had sold me the car he needed to get off his lot and had little care for what I wanted. Truthfully, I didn't know exactly what I wanted in a car; I left that choice to the car dealer. Now, when I go to purchase a car and the car salesmen swarms me as I come in, I take control. I encourage mentees to take control as well when faced by unscrupulous and persuasive recruiters. College recruiters have all the tricks of the trade to convince a young inexperienced person into believing their school should be the athlete's choice. Young people need to realize, it's merely a sales pitch. When a car salesman says, "Can I help you?" before the sales pitch begins I say, yes and I begin to describe in great detail exactly what I'm looking for. The moral of my story is that mentees need to have a good idea of what they want in choosing a school, car or anything else. I would always say to my mentees, *Do some research, look beyond the obvious. Otherwise, you could be very disappointed with what a stranger can decide for you."*

When guiding young people toward their college journey, my role as a mentor was to provide them with the tools to make their own choice. Challenging them to think critically about the decision to attend college and everything weighted in that decision. Encouraging them to question their possibilities as a way of exploration and discovery. I directed mentees to create a list of potential colleges and include a "reach" school. What am I looking for in a college or university? What's best for my future? Do they have my specific area of interest? Private versus public institution? Remember, turn over every stone to be safe and sure.

Mentoring taught me, when sharing time, experiences and providing a good process, mentees have a favorable chance of making a positive decision. Once the mentee has a solid technique to make choices, we gain comfort in their decisions, whatever those may be. Assist them in building a blueprint to follow and they can fill in their dreams. Ultimately, it is their ability to make solid choices that will matter.

CHAPTER IX
ROUNDING THE BASES

There is something to be said about new beginnings; a fresh start. I envisioned this new opportunity of becoming the Assistant Basketball Coach at Northern Illinois University to be an exciting new beginning for myself. I truly began to embrace the thought of major change in my life. My heart was open and my mind was changing focus. It was a very special time in my life.

With time now taking care of the transition, I began to focus on my new position. This job was a calling, a clear yet untraveled path for me to follow. The timing felt impeccable for my career. Building relationships with the college athletes and the challenge of recruiting young people was exciting and different. With most situations in my life, I gravitate toward digging deep into the challenge. This opportunity would be no different. Observe and study the very specifics of the job, be open minded and develop solid relationships and work to become the best in the business. This I deemed a very successful formula for winning!

In my discussions and research concerning my new position, I was informed of possible pitfalls;previous coaches and alums who I polled, shared stories of racism that I may face at NIU. The trials of racism were nothing new in my world; my past experiences prepared me for these issues. I did my due diligence in finding out the history that preceded me and the current issues I would potentially encounter. In the 22 years that I was an administrator at NIU, there were never any glaring issues of racism that I encountered. I believe that the tide was shifting when I arrived on campus. Nevertheless, I was always aware of the climate and the potential to stand ready as an activist for change for people of color should the need arise.

Dr. Deacon Davis, an accomplished African American, had been chosen by then NIU President Rhoten Smith, to be the Director of Special Programs. In that position, Deacon established the "Chance Program". This program focused on recruiting, admitting and assisting students who showed promise for succeeding in college, despite limited preparation and resources. During my tenure, the university named an annual award in his name for his relentless service. That year, I was the proud recipient of the award. Established in 1968, this program continues to thrive, some 50 plus years later, due to the continued successes of those who otherwise would have not been admitted. His service to others has been rewarded by the renaming of the program, The McKinley"Deacon"Davis Chance Program.

Johnny Butler, an outstanding coach, mentor and trailblazer, who I mentioned earlier had also been an assistant coach prior to my arrival. He was involved in a sit-in during a basketball game that exposed many grievances of the minority population. He was able to mediate with all parties to help bring the situation to a positive resolve. Students were heard and new proposals were put in place. Both of these trailblazers inspired me to pick up the torch and continue the fight for justice for students of color. I acknowledged that this plight reached well beyond the confines of coaching. I was now another Black face of hope for the minority college community.

First day on the job wasn't quite your normal first day. There were photo shoots for the new staff, a media luncheon and many questions to answer. In the midst of meeting boosters, support staff etc. one person in particular stood out to me- an amazing African American man named Walter Owens. He seemingly waltzed into my world. He served as assistant basketball coach prior to becoming the head baseball coach at NIU. His background also included high school coaching in Detroit, which was all similar to my path. He had played in the Negro Leagues, which fascinated my interest. Somehow his shoes began to fit my feet; he was a beacon of hope for me. Walter Owens had worn the shoes I was about to put on and committed himself to helping me find my way. He agreed to mentor me and I am proud to mention, he remains my mentor even after his passing. I'll never forget the moments when I felt overwhelmed on my journey. Walter always had a story or thought that could reshape the situation. His shared stories lifted me when things got heavy. Mentors have that, almost sudden impact for recharging batteries.

For the most part, I felt at home and unbridled by the underlying racism. After all it wasn't my first rodeo when it came to this ugliness. I was up for the challenge;it was time to take hold of the reins from these great men. I concluded you can't win if you're not challenged.

Amongst the constant challenges the opportunity to coach and mentor kept me in a favored position to serve others. As I've gazed in reverse, service to others has always brought great satisfaction to my spirit.

Northern Illinois University suddenly became my main focus. My juices really began to flow with each passing day. I was fully committed to making this work. There is something to be said about small, significant change. For example, the professional dress code for the NIU men's basketball staff initially presented a challenge for me. I was accustomed to wearing warm up suits and sneakers when coaching and teaching physical education classes. Now, in my new role at NIU, my wardrobe underwent an upgrade; I traded in my relaxed attire for a more professional look, a suit and tie was what was expected of me. I made the adjustment and I strongly encouraged my mentees to follow my lead and dress for success when interviewing for jobs or attending public gatherings etc. You only get one opportunity to make a good first impression. Your appearance tells a quick at-a-glance story of who you are, how confident you are and that you are serious about the business at hand. I always told my mentees to take great pride in how they present themselves. That little bit of effort will get you respect and pay off in dividends. Winners dress for success!

Coaching and mentoring college athletes began immediately upon my arrival at NIU. Our first team meetings consisted of getting acquainted with the returning players. Some of the returnees were somewhat hesitant to trust the new staff. From that beginning, I felt my coaching background gave me a bit of leverage with many of the players. I had read the profiles of many of them during their high school careers, so talking, sharing stories and listening to their issues seemed to ignite a connection.

College life was a whole new world for the incoming Freshman athletes. They had to adjust to the major change in leadership and the fact that the coaches and staff that previously recruited them were no longer available to guide them. It was imperative that trust be established in order to get full cooperation and buy-in. I would mingle with the young men to simply understand how life was for them as student athletes. I visited with them in their dorms and even stopped in the dining halls for quick chats. These small gestures really began the process of trust, and quickly put me in good favor with them. Being able to relate meant I could secure greater cooperation when asking for their best efforts in the classroom and on the basketball floor. I actually enjoyed getting to know the young men.

When you coach and mentor student athletes, or any young person for that matter, they need to believe that you genuinely care about their lives. As mentors, we need to be patient and understand that the college world is a new way of life for these young men. Some will adjust quickly, and others may struggle... At the high school level, I had coached and mentored young men who had similar backgrounds with one another. This gave me a slight advantage; I was familiar with the walks of life from which they came, only now, they weren't high school athletes, they were college athletes. Recruiting athletes from the talent rich Chicago Public Schools and the Catholic League was of utmost importance to our future success. My immediate attention and focus was now very pointed; our first recruiting class would no doubt decide if we sank or swam. After evaluating our roster and talent currently in place, we realized what was needed for the future and set out to find those athletes who fit our profile. With talent being first, academic standing, character and enthusiasm for the game were of high priority. We shared our priorities with recruits and they quickly understood that talent is very important, but other factors can sometimes be the deciding factor for who is offered these highly cherished scholarships. I believed in sharing the truth when it came to what our expectations were.

While seeking the best student athletes, I reached out to many coaches I knew in the area. Many were very helpful mainly because they were familiar with my reputation and trusted that I would do what was best for their athletes.

There were a few hesitations, for one reason or another, but for the most part, our staff had success in our recruiting efforts. We were successful in recruiting several of the area's finest athletes. The high school round ballers (aka basketball players)we targeted were from the inner city of Chicago- a high priority for us. Their work ethic which encompassed toughness, competitiveness and a great desire to excel, fit the mold we were looking for. The combined talent of these young men meshed well together. Ultimately, during their time at NIU, they acquired successful careers culminating in a league championship and a trip to the very prestigious NCAA Men's Basketball Tournament.

Strangely enough, as I got to know these young men during the recruiting process and their early college years, I discovered that their needs were uniquely different. That discovery made mentoring somewhat complex. Mentoring athletes is not a *"cookie cutter situation"*. Each person is uniquely gifted and different even though they may share similar issues.

One similarity was the fact that most of these young men were raised by Black, single parent mothers. Without the presence of a strong and positive male role-model in their lives,raising a young Black man single handedly was a very difficult task, even for an able-bodied, hardworking and energetic woman. I can recall a few mothers who would tell me, *"Coach Collins, when I leave my home to go to work in the morning, he is asleep. When I come home from my second job he's asleep. The times in between, I hope you are making sure he is doing the right thing!" I could only reply, "Yes ma'am, I got you!"* As their mentor, I took that responsibility very seriously. I saw first hand how important my role was to these mothers.

Unfortunately, single parenting was somewhat commonplace, as I had experienced this phenomenon many times during my teaching and coaching at the elementary and high school level. Adversely, not many dads attended the games. Working with these young athletes became a labor of love for me as I was thrust into being that male role-model that these mothers had wanted and desired for their sons. I can honestly say I loved those kids as if they were my own. That was one reason why I took that position quite seriously; I really respected the sacrifices and challenges these strong Black mothers faced.

For me, the greatest reward of recruiting was getting to know young people and contributing to their efforts to become the best they could possibly be. Providing them with support and knowledge was fulfilling. I saw in those single mothers' eyes what they wanted for their sons and never lost sight of that. Yes, I loved and needed to win basketball games, it was the basis of my job and I loved the thrill. Yet, mentoring these young men for the game of life became just as significant if not more important than a basketball game. When I got to really engage these young men and actually feel the hopeful heartbeats of their beloved parents, I developed a greater understanding of my own self-worth. The games, win or lose, may or may not be remembered, but the lessons learned, experiences shared and who these young people ultimately became in life made an indelible mark upon my heart.

One way in which I attempted to expand the knowledge of my mentees was by allowing them to experience the beauty of new horizons. Obviously, we had their attention with basketball, so we dangled that carrot and led them to places and experiences they had never been before. Exposing them to a whole new world beyond their own community was the experience I yearned for them to have; so many of these young men had such limited exposure to the world. Trips downtown, for example, were a rarity for many. The local neighborhood parks and playgrounds were their daily stomping grounds. Now, as a Division One athlete, traveling out of state for games was always a great experience and an opportunity to experience places they had only read about in books and magazines. Astonishingly, most of these young men had never flown on an airplane! Being a college athlete now afforded them the opportunity to play ball in places like Miami, Florida, California and much of the Midwest. On road trips, we would often book a tour of the city to add to their experience, exposure and knowledge. Besides their regular weekly studies, we would provide life skills sessions featuring etiquette classes, guest speakers, hospital and local school visits or whatever I deemed as productive or life changing for these young men. We wanted them to see the broader picture of themselves and life because the reality would soon hit them that one day the basketball will eventually stop bouncing. They needed to envision their future and the many possibilities after a career in basketball.

I loved winning! I loved grabbing the first place trophy when earned, but the bigger win was seeing young people flourish, not only on the court but also in life. Mentoring assisted these young people into becoming well-rounded individuals. Guiding them and exposing them to the possibilities in the world was potentially life-changing during these very critical years in their lives. That is my way to spell Win!

After my first year as Assistant Coach at NIU, I felt I had a solid handle on the methods of recruiting and identifying talent. I was also extremely confident in my abilities to communicate with recruits, coaches and parents, which was a very important skill to possess. I truly believed honesty and integrity were the main ingredients for much of our success. Parents and those involved in the recruiting process respected our methods and the way in which we carried ourselves. Recruiting could be a messy endeavor, but we took pride and did things the right way.

I observed and read about college coaches who cut corners and were not always straightforward about their true intentions. The very first day I took that position, I decided I would only operate above board and by the book. No recruit was worth tarnishing my reputation, it was all I had. I wanted to be known to the professionals in my field that I did things the right way.

Charlie Smith was one of the finest young men I had the opportunity to coach during my high school tenure. He was an excellent student-athlete, polite and very respectful, and not to mention, an extremely talented basketball player. He was that all-American boy you'd like your daughter to bring home. His loving parents deserve total credit. They conceived 13 children! Charlie was number 12 in the line-up. That achievement is only surpassed by the fact that they all graduated from college. Each of them were respectful and very successful, as their mother ran a tight, disciplined ship. All of the children were goal-oriented and steadfast in their approach. Their living quarters were tucked away in the basement with beds made like soldiers; the area was as clean as a whistle.

On the night that Charlie was to sign his national letter of intent to attend college, everyone was set to gather at his home for the event. This was a huge deal for a young man from the Englewood community, on Chicago's southside. His mom had prepared a Thanksgiving type meal to celebrate the occasion. It was truly the makings of a joyful moment for this young man who had worked so hard for this opportunity. His new coaches were to arrive at six that evening for the signing, but sadly enough, they never showed or called. Needless to say, I was not happy. Charlie was devastated. That was the first time I saw a tear fall from his eyes. The family was confused and very disappointed. What do I say? What do I do? I was at a loss for any good explanation. His mom, being the God fearing person that she was, made the best comment when she said, "Charlie, it just wasn't meant to be." Being at a loss for words, everyone agreed on that fact and we decided this had all happened for a reason; we would wait and see what the coming days had in store. We smiled, said a prayer and enjoyed those tasty desserts his mom had prepared.

Charlie's value took less than twenty four hours to realize; the word was out. Charlie Smith had not signed a letter of intent to attend Wichita State University. Early that next day, I received a phone call from Boyd Grant, the head basketball coach at Fresno State University. Without hesitation, Coach Grant offered Charlie a full scholarship to attend Fresno! This special young man from the very tough inner city community of Englewood had struck gold. When you survive the streets of Englewood you have accomplished a great deal. Gangs, drugs and trouble crossed his path, but Charlie remained focused and determined to make good on his dreams. As a mentor and coach, I was very proud to associate with this special young man.

Charlie went on to Fresno State, where he had a tremendous career, and continues to reside in Fresno, California. He earned a degree in Business Administration with an emphasis in Marketing. Charlie was certainly a memorable experience for me, but there were many mentees/players with somewhat similar stories and experiences over the years that I have cherished and have fond memories of. Today, I still enjoy the many spontaneous calls I get from ex players and mentees I was privileged to mentor- especially around the holidays….. priceless!

CHAPTER X
WELCOME TO THE BIG LEAGUES

Coaching and mentoring people like Charlie, Alfrederick, Smokey and so many others was a lifetime of great experiences and if I could do it all over again, I surely would. As life would have it, there was still more, much more of God's plan in store for me. I felt with each step, God had presented lessons along the way to prepare me for the next. I was actually being prepped for something that was not on my bucket list.

My journey had now become pretty extensive. The elementary and high school portion of my professional journey(which covered the first fifteen years of my career) had accumulated many unforgettable memories. As I moved to college level coaching for six seasons, these memories and experiences as well, had really begun to mount.

Just when you think your path has revealed a straightforward road, suddenly there are bends and turns just ahead. Things may slow down at first, but as I turned the corners and got around the bends, there were new unforeseen challenges and opportunities awaiting me.

I always reminded my mentees, as well as my own son, that you never know who's watching you and over the years, they have found that to be true. During my tenure as assistant basketball coach at NIU, there was someone watching me. I found out later that they saw more than a basketball coach; they saw a greater value with my skill set. After leaving NIU and spending three years as assistant basketball coach at DePaul University, in my mind, my next step was to become a Division I Basketball Coach; that was the goal I set my sights on. However, that's where the road began to turn.

Having led two national top ten recruiting classes, my stock quickly rose. I was considered one of the top assistant coaches in the country. We signed Howard Nathan, otherwise known as *Mr. Basketball*, from Peoria Manual High School in Peoria, IL. Mr. Basketball is a title given to outstanding player of the year. We also signed the runner-up, Tom Kleininschmidt, from Chicago's Gordon Tech High School. Those efforts afforded me a few interviews for Division I head coaching jobs. I was now in a good position; my hard work was paying off.

At that particular time, there were very few Black Division I head coaches- they could actually be counted on one hand. I realized some of my interviews were strictly tokenism, which was a very hard pill for me to swallow. Predominately White Institutions (PWIs) were being pressured to interview and hire minority prospects, due to the lack of diversity in college basketball coaching. Even though I was qualified for the

position, the odds of actually getting hired was slim to none.
After that particular hiring period, I came up empty. I was
very, very disappointed. I couldn't or maybe I just didn't want
to understand how things really were. I watched younger, less
qualified white coaches be thrust into these great jobs. I can't
lie, I felt unsupported by my white boss; I felt he should have
pushed harder for me. He clearly could have made a difference,
but he chose not to, for whatever reason. I really began to
question why I would want to continue on this road. Seemingly,
no one noticed these travesties and the disservice to Black
coaches in general. I wasn't the only Black assistant coach to
feel this way. Sadly, my dream of becoming a Division I head
coach was fading away...

   After learning that my last (possible) interview didn't yield the
results I desired, I felt the need to be alone. I went to my office
at DePaul and literally got down on my knees- which actually
felt very weak at that moment. I had no one to share with how
I felt and I was too embarrassed to even complain. The staff
I was working with at that time was all white - they were the
last people I wanted to see; I knew I didn't have their support.
While on my knees, I began to pray the 23rd Psalm, the same
psalm my dad prayed while stranded in the dense jungle of
Bouganville. In that moment, I thought of him. I thought about
the trials and barriers my idol Jackie Robinson, and many other
Black men who had been slighted because of the color of their
skin, had to endure. Somehow, praying and thinking of them
began to strengthen me. My weak knees and my fatigued

spirit, got a charge. Before rising, I asked my Lord and Savior to lift me up and place me where I could do more to serve Him. The realization had come:I could no longer be of service where I currently was. There had to be a better way for me, there just had to be!

There will come a time when you yearn for something so bad, but it escapes you. You won't understand it then, but soon enough you will come to realize that which you desperately yearned for, wasn't meant for you. Earlier, I mentioned that you never know who's watching you. This is true. As I've expressed before, I've always encouraged my mentees, in everything you do to come with your "A-Game." Whether you like it or not, someone is always watching you. Since they're going to observe, wow them with your best!

While at NIU, the Athletics Administration Department had observed other skills and abilities that I possessed and just happened to reach out. It had been less than two months after my prayer moment, when I asked GOD to move in a mighty way in my life. Daily, I had continued to pray the desires of my heart knowing that patience would be essential. My faith, at that point, kept me in a positive and confident state. I just knew something would soon change, because the GOD who is always watching knew where he wanted me to be.

Ironically, I received a call from the Athletics Director at NIU where I had previously worked. After a brief chat, he said, "*Robert I would like for you to interview for the position of Associate Athletics Director here at NIU.*" My first thought was, another token interview! I knew their only African American associate was leaving, so I must have had "token" written across my forehead. That position was absolutely not what I was searching for. He offered more details on the position, but in my mind, I just never saw a fit for me, after all I was a basketball coach, not an administrator. I politely declined the offer. I never had a second thought about the job until three days later when he called again. After some small talk, he approached me one more time with his ask: *"Are you sure you wouldn't want to just interview for the job?"* Without taking too much of his time, I repeated my decision, thanked him once again and ended the conversation. I may have had some lingering second thoughts, but I still was not moved by the offer. I hadn't really discussed the matter with anyone, so I decided to reach out to a mentor of mine, Dr Jacquline Simmons, the Principal from Robeson High School. I trusted and respected her immensely. Dr. Simmons provided me with a different perspective on the situation. In her calm, methodical approach, she began to point out things I hadn't thought about in regards to the job offer, and my future plans. After listening to my reasons for turning down the job, she asked me one question: *"Tell me what your dream is for your future?"* Without hesitation I replied, " *I'd actually like to become a Division I Head Basketball Coach and win a National Championship."* She then said, *"That sounds great, but after that, then what? "* I hadn't really given that question much thought. I appreciated her insight; she had rattled my thought process and made me take a hard look at myself. After a short pause, I said, *"I'll probably pursue Athletics Administration."* After a brief pause, she just kinda smiled when she saw the lights, bells and whistles going off in my head. It was an aha-moment! Before she could say another word, I knew what she was thinking. She didn't have to spell out the obvious to me, she just kinda nudged me along the path. Then, with a look of assurance and wisdom, Dr. Simmons said, *"Mr. Collins, sometimes things don't come as we plan. Your plan seemed right, but you're a Black man in a white environment. This may just be the opportunity you have been seeking after all. It just may be coming sooner than you anticipated. I advise you to take a second look, just to be sure."*

On my ride home, I thought carefully about all I had just ingested. Amazingly enough, that very next day, I got another call from the Athletics director's secretary who said he would like to meet with me face-to-face and he wouldn't take no for an answer. I was now better equipped to make an informed decision. We met at Papa Bears, a small breakfast place just off the highway. During our meeting, the athletics director began to point out duties, opportunities, perks and other facets of the job that I was unfamiliar with, nevertheless, I found intriguing. It wasn't until he said, *"Look at it this way Robert, you will be coaching coaches and be responsible for some 400 hundred athletes!"* Bingo! For some reason, that struck a chord in my gut. Suddenly, I began to see the plan GOD had for me. I began to feel that this opportunity had my name on it; it was mine for the taking. I responded,, *"Let me sleep on it and I'll give you a call in the morning with my final answer."*

That night, as I was speaking with close family members about the opportunity, I realized I was taking basketball coaching off my plate- probably for good. I let that sink in for a moment... It was actually the toughest portion of this equation. With Dr. Simmons' enlightening conversation ringing in my head, I had come to another life-changing moment. With butterflies in my stomach and still tons of uncertainties looming in the distance, I made the call and accepted the job of Associate Athletics Director at NIU! The opportunity to mentor young adult coaches and hundreds of aspiring athletes would allow me to cast a wider net. My adrenaline was flowing! Suddenly, I felt optimistic about the future.

Armed with many skills and attributes acquired along the way, I began my migration to NIU Athletics as Associate Athletics Director. Challenged by multiple issues that a multitude of young people faced, I set out to design a program to effectively fit the vast majority.

I mentored volleyball players, gymnasts, wrestlers, baseball players, inner city football and basketball athletes-all from different ethnic backgrounds and communities, but their basic goal was the same: enjoy college athletics while pursuing a college degree. Sounds simple, but there were pitfalls along the way.

I discovered that for the most part, these young people lacked information on collegic academia, what it takes to become a successful athlete and how to navigate life on a college campus. I determined that my job was to prepare them for the real world, while providing a world class experience. I had to squeeze into their few "free time" hours and work to refine independent living skills as well as create opportunities for them to practice the life skills they learned. Their professors demanded their best efforts mentally, while their coaches expected maximum physical effort. Time management and other responsibilities of being a student athlete were daunting; there was quite a bit of heavy lifting involved and many times without much needed resources.

The American college experience, as we know it, is not limited to rigorous study. There is also the social aspect of college life. Students have the opportunity to engage in an array of social activities such as intramural sports,cultural and political organizations, fraternities and sororities, the arts and much more! Most young people are not accustomed to the new found freedom of college life; finding the balance between academia and social life can be tricky, at best. Without a good plan and some support in place, your average student athlete will find themselves struggling to maintain some sense of balance; academics and athletic performance can decline rapidly. Our athletics staff consistently provided resources and information at conventions and mini seminars during the school year in order to support our student athletes.

There were serious issues that arose from time to time that ultimately impacted a student and the department in a negative way. Each student athlete was made aware of the Athletics

Department and the University's Code of Conduct and zero tolerance where issues such as drug and alcohol abuse, date rape, hazing to name a few were concerned. The athletes were constantly reminded, especially the underclassman, of these potential *"pitfalls"* and the subsequent severe consequences that follow misconduct. I always told the students *"I can't, nor do I want to be with you during your weekend fun times, but what I do want you to understand is that your actions during that time need to be smart choices!"*

With that in mind, I developed a bright red card, the size of a credit card, that they were required to carry with them at all times. We called it our "Smart Card", a simple reminder of their responsibilities to make solid choices. Their team, their family, their reputations were on the line. Just knowing they carried that card as a reminder, actually comforted me and gave them some accountability to themselves. Monday mornings became less of a problem as weekend trouble became almost non-existent. Young people will make good choices when they have solid mentoring.

Unfortunately (as I've said before) you can't save everyone, but our life skills program and the presence of good mentors annually increased our success rate. The athletes actually began to take great pride in themselves; they wanted their image to be one of campus leaders, not just athletes.

For young people to thrive and prosper, positive leadership and the presence of a caring mentor can be priceless.

CHAPTER XI
PEANUTS & CRACKERJACKS

The great novelist and activist James Baldwin once said, *"Children have never been good at listening to their elders, but they never fail to imitate them."*

Without a doubt, each and every one of us is a flawed human being. But in the eyes of the mentee, his or her mentor is pure perfection. Mentors mold, shape, guide and yes, model for the mentee what their life could be, which is why it is most important to be mindful of the image we present to our young mentees.

My elders lived by the saying, *"Baseball is as American as apple pie!"* When I think of baseball, apple pie isn't the image that comes to my mind. Yet I do think of my favorite ballpark treat, Cracker Jacks, inspired by the song, *"Take Me Out to the Ballgame".* Cracker Jacks, that tasty, caramel corn and nuts that came with a prize in every box- that was a real staple for me.

With that said, I'd like to share with you some staples for coaching and mentoring young people that will be helpful. Consider the following:

- Embody a positive, uplifting mind set.
- Always operate with Honesty and Integrity.
- Lead with an open and sincere heart.
- Show up! Physical presence says, *"I'm here for you."*
- Actively listen and then, listen some more.
- Avoid judging at all cost.

For a mentor, these points will always be cutting edge, but like anything else, research articles on mentoring, read stories and seek other mentoring techniques as a way for continued personal growth and development. Always keep an eye out for young, bright potential mentors- we can never have too many. Mentors are of great value to our society today. A sincere heart makes all the other points come together; sincerity is like love, everybody needs it.

Having a successful career speaks for itself. When asked about their personal aspirations, often times I would hear mentees say, *"I want to be like you Mr. Collins."* I was flattered, no doubt, but I always encouraged my mentees to develop their own sense of identity and follow their own course; my path was uniquely meant for me as their path would be of their own making.

Looking back on a successful career, I don't see myself, I see those I served, and those who created and paved my way. I see those who mentored me and those who depended on me. That's just how I see it! "How do *you* spell win?"

CHAPTER XII
MY FIELD OF DREAMS
(TESTIMONIALS)

Throughout my fabulous journey, I was blessed to meet so many amazing people. Having mentioned so many instances and experiences with mentees, I wanted to share a few of their testimonials.

Testimonial by **Rodney Davis**

I first crossed paths with Robert Collins in (August 1983) when as a high school athlete, I participated in the Nike AFBE Camp at the University of Iowa. Fast forward to four years later when I actually met Coach Collins; he was the Assistant Men's Basketball Coach at Northern Illinois University in DeKalb, IL. where I was a student athlete. Coach Collins came to NIU when I was in my junior year. His focus was on rebuilding the program. I was not recruited by Coach Collins or his team and that reality created some anxiety for me and my returning teammates. I wondered, would we get a fair chance to prove ourselves worthy of playing for a guy that I was not recruited by?

Well, the answer for me was, yes!

Coach Collins was fair, honest, and demanding. He challenged me to be better on the court, in the classroom, and in life. Coach Collins and I have built an incredible bond that has continued far beyond my days of playing basketball. Coach is a person that loves to share his experiences and assist young people to avoid the pitfalls in life.

Coach, I love you and appreciate you! Although I may not have been one of your original recruits, I know that still, to this very day, I can say that I have a true mentor and friend for life. Congratulations on your book. I can't wait to read it!

Testimonial by Leon Ellis

I thank God for Coach Collins being in my life. Ever since the day we met, he believed in me, even when I didn't believe in myself. My family life was very dysfunctional, which at times left me feeling less than hopeful. The mentoring, love and support I received from Coach Collins bought me hope. He encouraged me to put my best foot forward and reach high.

I encountered some difficult legal challenges during my adult life. Yet during those times, Coach Collins never passed judgement on me, even when family members doubted me. When I was exonerated, he made the comment, "You can never keep a good man down!" That was a lesson he taught me back in high school and it resonated with me during my legal battle.

Thanks Coach! I'm blessed to have you in my life.

Testimonial by Darrell Hill

Robert Collins is a person I have a tremendous amount of respect for. I attended NIU from 1998 to 2001 on a football scholarship. Navigating your way through the muddy waters of college athletics can be very difficult; I realized right away it was no longer high school- there was so much more at stake. Coaches and athletic administrator's jobs depended on the performance of young student athletes. To be 100% honest, the NIU Coaching staff was not concerned much about the players on a personal level. Most players like myself felt like we had no one to talk to when times were rough in our personal lives or on the football field. Especially the African American players. At least until we met Mr. Collins. Mr. Collins let it be known from day 1 that his door was always open if we had any problems, needed any advice, or just needed someone to talk to. A lot people would say that, but Mr. Collins really meant it. Mr. Collins was always transparent, honest, and genuine. He gave so much wisdom, and guidance. He held us accountable. He demanded excellence from us academically, personally and athletically. He had the ability to help you see the positive side of any situation. He was a true mentor, advocate, and leader. I am forever grateful for the impact he had on my life.

Testimonial by Alfrederick Hughes

The first time I met Coach Collins was under a series of very uncomfortable circumstances. Someone very close to me had recently passed away and I was also feeling the weight of the notoriety of being a high school basketball star. To compound matters, I was to be the starting Forward for the Robeson Raiders, however, Coach Collins had the grim task of telling me I was to be sidelined until my grades improved. When he informed me that I was unable to play, I literally hated his guts (I shared this statement of fact with him many years later). At some point, I realized he was trying to support me and not humiliate me. That realization gained my respect for him.

I have grown to love and respect Coach Collins, and I share that with him each time we communicate. Coach Collins taught me to be a man! He modeled for me a healthy image of what it meant to be a man. I was reluctant to change, but he gently pulled me in and showed me the way. Plain and simple, I never would have made it without Coach Collins.

Testimonial by **Antwon Johnson**

I remember the fall of 1989 at NIU (Northern Illinois University). Robert Collins, affectionately known as COACH C, was overseeing our study hall. Another teammate and I decided we would ditch study hall and go to the dorm to watch the Chicago Bulls play the Detroit Pistons. While joyfully watching the Bulls beat their rival the Pistons, there was a knock on the door. Thinking it was one of our teammates, we opened the door and to our surprise, there was Coach C. His only words were "Meet me at the fieldhouse at 5:30am for punishment." My roommate and I were afraid of what lies ahead for us the next morning, so much so that we didn't sleep all night. The next day, we arrived at the fieldhouse at 5:30am. Coach C met us at the door and sat us down to talk. I will always remember what he expressed to us during that conversation. "Son, in life you have a chance to make a good choice, a bad choice or the right choice and because you made a bad choice, I have to make the right choice for you". He proceeded to run the crap out of us for one and a half hours. After we finished with the running and were heading back to the dorm, he said, "I still love you guys and expect so much more from you". Needless to say, we never skipped study hall again. Now, as a coach myself, I appreciate Coach Collins so much more. Everything that he taught me about life resonates with me today as a coach and mentor for young adults. Thank you Coach C for loving me unconditionally. I hope I have made you proud!

Testimonial by Clark "Smokey" Morgan

I met Robert Collins in 1971 – I was 13 yrs. old and a student at Avalon Park Elementary School in Chicago, Illinois. He was my gym teacher and basketball coach. He set the standard for our basketball team; he helped to guide our paths for what was next in life's journey. Even after that time was over, Robert continued to mentor many of us throughout our life's journey. After high school, I attended and graduated from Eastern Illinois University and became a teacher with the Chicago Public Schools. It was because of Mr. Collins that I had a great tenure at Westinghouse High School in Chicago, IL., where

I was not only a Physical Education Teacher, but became the Dean of Students and Athletic Director. To this day, I credit my successful career to the guidance and love I received from Mr. Collins outside of my mom's and dad's home. He helped me realize that there is more to life than just hanging out with the "fellas." He understood young adults and talked to us about the realities that we will face as Black men in the real world.

Today, I am 62 years of age, and can tenderly say that you played a major role in me becoming the husband, father, grandfather and man that I am today. Coach, thank you for seeing the potential that I had to be better, and also seeing the potential of greatness in all young people. Blessings to you, Coach!

Testimonial by Gloria Reeves

I am so elated to have an opportunity to speak about a man that I truly respect. This man, Robert Collins, changed my life in such a meaningful way.

As our friendship developed during our teaching together, he asked me if I would consider coaching the girl's basketball team at Beasley Academic Center where we both taught. I immediately responded by saying I don't know anything about coaching. He insisted that he could teach me everything that I needed to know to be a successful coach. After coaching the girls at Beasley for a year, upon Robert's suggestion, I applied for the coaching position at Robeson

High School where he coached the boys. Initially, I didn't get the position, but a year later, I applied again and was hired! After being mentored by Mr. Collins, I developed into a coach to be reckoned with; Robert helped me develop into a Hall of Fame Coach. He was an excellent teacher and I was a motivated learner. Robert wasn't aware of this, but I was going through a lot in my life when I met him. Coaching gave my life purpose and created a new future for me- one that I would not have realized had it not been for Mr. Collins. I will forever be grateful to Mr. Robert Collins, my friend and mentor for life.

Testimonial by **Charlie Smith**

I will be forever grateful to my Mentor, Coach Robert Collins, for helping to change my life. I grew up on the south side of Chicago and I was the 12th of 13 children born to my parents. Life was challenging, yet I strived to be a good student-athlete and reach for my goals and dreams. The words of wisdom, teaching, coaching, work ethic, discipline, life skills, physical and mental training demands administered by Coach Robert Collins helped to mold me into an honor student, high school and college Hall of Fame Inductee, college graduate, business man, husband, father, and a productive role model citizen in society.

Testimonial by **Connie Teaberry**

To have a person believe in you before you have ever met them is a powerful feeling. Mr. Collins was extremely integral in me obtaining the Head Coach position at Northern Illinois University in December of 2004.. I had just accepted another coaching job when he called me to consider the NIU position. As a result, I've been in the position now for seventeen years, and recently earned a title change: Director of Cross Country, Track and Field. Mr. Collins' belief in me inspired me to succeed; I could not let him or myself down. His positive words, uplifting messages, and guiding advice has fed my soul, my children's soul and those of the student athletes I've had the pleasure of coaching. Mr. Collins made sure I understood my role and advised me on how to handle myself as an African American woman in a coaching world dominated by men. I felt I knew how to coach, but the business aspect that went with my title needed nurturing. Mr. Collins never micromanaged me, but instead allowed me to design the team with my vision, and was always there to help me find my way when I became unsure. He was always available to impart concrete ideas that helped me to develop my own style and way of doing things. He is relatable, which makes him extremely easy to talk to about just about anything. I am grateful that the Lord brought Mr. Collins into my life and I am proud to call him my mentor and friend.

Testimonial by Garrett Wolfe

As an African American male from the inner city of Chicago, it always felt good to know that I had someone who understood me and would help me to navigate my path. Mr. Collins was a positive influence in that his general disposition was always professional, precise, yet warm and comforting. He often offered me reassurance, which boosted my self-confidence and helped me to consider what it meant to be a leader. At times, when I was being taken advantage of and people were not being kind to me, Coach Collins came to my defence. He modeled how young, black men should conduct ourselves in public situations. He would most times wait with me while I got myself together after a game and before a press conference to ensure I didn't feel rushed while I got suited up; he and I shared the belief in making a great impression. For a time, I strongly considered pursuing a role in College Athletics; Coach Collins made the job appear seamless. I cannot count the times that he made himself available to my family and I- ways that far exceeded his role at NIU (wellness checks, funeral visits, etc..) Coach Collins was a guiding light in my life and so many others. I will always be forever grateful to him.

EXTRA INNINGS
(ACKNOWLEDGEMENTS)

How Do You Spell Win, says a few things to me when it comes to how I view life. Where winning is concerned, what's most important to you? The outcome, the prize or simply the experience? What do you value most in life? As a coach, I walked away with a few medals and trophies, but as I reflect on those material prizes, they were not what brought me a sense of joy and accomplishment. The relationships that were fostered, the sharing of life experiences, and the insurmountable life lessons learned, that was truly the ultimate prize; that's how I spell win, plain and simple! Over time,those trophies will tarnish and rust, but the positive experiences and the young people I had the opportunity to mentor have left an indelible mark upon my life forever more.

This book has been a dream of mine for quite some time and the reality of completion is amazingly fulfilling. This would not have been possible without the fabulous path God has guided me down. That path would not have been possible without a fabulous group of human beings I now consider to be an extension of my family: the elementary and high school teams I coached and the college student athletes I served. Thank you for letting me into your lives, as I hope and pray that my moments with you were meaningful and helpful.

I never considered that my book would reach the height of becoming a bestseller. I just always felt my journey was so purposeful it just might inspire or motivate someone else, if they simply read about it. We are not always born with what we need, we have to somehow acquire it. Mentoring makes these acquisitions possible. What personally motivated me to write this book was seeing the need for guidance with many of the young people I encountered; many young people didn't have a strong, male figure in their life to help guide their future. Without the presence of a positive role model, there is an increased likelihood of negative behaviors and outcomes that have the potential to lead to incarceration, early death, drug related failures and a multitude of unfortunate possibilities.

As many as 25 percent of children in the U.S. are parented by single mothers. That's 18 million children who do not have a father figure living in their household. Seventy-one percent of high school dropouts who have trouble academically and socially are fatherless.

Love and praise to those closest to my heart, my children: Dori, Ria, Paige and Bobby. They provided the strength I needed to complete this project.

I'd like to acknowledge these very special people and groups who contributed to my journey. Thank You for your portion. Together we will never forget our moments.

Dr. Samuel Abernathy

Ms. Edris Adams

Tony Adams

The Beasley Academic Center

Ms. Monique Bernoudy

Elizabeth Berquist

My Calvary Church Usher Team

Bobby Cesarek

The Colby Twins

Larry Cole

Timm Collier and remembrance of brothers Lou, Bey and Bobby

Phillip Cooper (deceased)

My Cuzzies

Richard E. "Daddio" Dailey (deceased)

Brooke Dodson

Lora and Mattie Dortch

Arthur Downer (deceased)

Edye Ellis

Jesse Fields

Mrs. Eleanor Fleming

The Graham Family (in memory of Russ)

Louis C. Gross, II and Family

Thomas Hammock

Ron Harris

LaShawn Johnson

Michael Lawson

Dwight Lewis

Walter Lewis

Ralph Miller

Harold Mitchell

Ashley Morrow

The 2003 NIU Football Team

Mike Nelson

Joe Novak

My Historic 21 brothers of Omega Psi Phi INC

Dr. James Phillips

Dr. Carrie Preston (deceased)

George Pruitt (deceased)

Charles Redmond (deceased)

1984 Robeson High School Basketball Team

Francine St. Claire

Alfred Simms

George T. Simms (deceased)

Megan Sprangers

Otis & Mike Traylor

Mike Turner

Pam Tyska

Tenisha Wilkins

Garrett Wolfe

Dr. Floyd Wyrick

Probably left off a few. Just too many to mention! Apologies....drop mic!